MONEY WI$E

Dennis Hensley

HARVEST HOUSE PUBLISHERS
Eugene, Oregon 97402

MONEY WISE

Copyright © 1991 by Dennis Hensley
Published by Harvest House Publishers
Eugene, Oregon 97402

Library of Congress Cataloging-in-Publication Data

Hensley, Dennis E., 1948–
　　Money wise / by Dennis Hensley.
　　ISBN 0-89081-863-0
　　1. Finance, Personal—Religious aspects—Christianity　　I. Title.
　HG179.H43　　　1991
　332.024—dc20　　　　　　　　　　　　　　　　　　　90-23595
　　　　　　　　　　　　　　　　　　　　　　　　　　　　　CIP

Printed in the United States of America.

*This book is dedicated to
Jim Schweickart and Steve Summers,
my business partners and
brothers in Christ.*

CONTENTS

Chapter 1

When Poverty Kicked My Teeth In

I grew up in a Christian family and I can't remember many Sundays when we weren't all seated in our regular pew at church listening to the sermon of the week. Adding 52 Sunday morning sermons to another 52 Sunday evening sermons, that made 104 sermons per year. Multiply that times the 40 years I've been alive and you come up with 4160 sermons. Now add to that at least 3500 more sermons I've listened to on Wednesday nights at prayer meetings, at weddings and funerals I've attended, at Good Friday and other special holiday services I've attended, and on radio and cassette tapes I've listened to, and you get 7660 sermons.

That's a lot of preaching, isn't it? In that vast range of sermons it would seem that I surely would have heard a message on just about everything there is to preach about.

But that isn't the case.

I never once saw a pastor stand before a congregation and announce, "My sermon topic today is 'How and Why Christians Should Become Independently Wealthy.'"

And that's really too bad, because somewhere along the line I needed to hear a sermon like that. If I had, I might have been spared the financial tragedy that struck me in 1978.

I came home from Vietnam in December 1971, after two years of service in the U.S. Army as a chaplain's assistant with the Armor Corps and later the Military Police. In April 1972 I was married to my college sweetheart. Rose had a good job as an elementary school teacher, so I decided to use the G.I. Bill to attend graduate school full-time in order to complete my M.A. degree in English. My intention was to one day become a professional writer, so this was good training. Eleven months later I had completed the degree. Great progress, right?

During this time Rose and I were living a comfortable life. We had rented a nice apartment and had bought ourselves several rooms of new furniture. We also had purchased all new appliances. We had even special-ordered a new car with a V-8 engine and dozens of fancy options. We ate out at restaurants or fast-food places at least three times each week. We took a cross-country vacation from Michigan to California and back, making every tourist stop from the Cowboy Hall of Fame in Oklahoma to Disneyland in California. We later took other vacations to the Smoky Mountains, to New Orleans, and to Michigan's Upper Peninsula. Life was terrific, and we gave very little thought to saving money. Why should we? I eventually landed a good job as an office manager with an electric company and Rose continued her teaching. If we seemed to be spending a lot, what did it matter? After all, we were making a lot.

By 1974, however, we decided that if I really wanted to become a successful author, I needed to go back to college and complete a Ph.D. in English. So Rose took a leave of absence from the school where she taught and I quit my office job and we moved to Muncie, Indiana, where I enrolled at Ball State University in the doctoral program in English.

To say that our lifestyle changed radically would be the understatement of the century. We used our severance paychecks, our checking account money, and another thousand dollars that I borrowed from my father to scrape together enough money to put a down payment on a small home (our first). I still had two years left to draw G.I. schooling benefits and the university was paying me a small stipend to teach one course of freshman composition each semester. Combined, however, these amounts did not exceed $6250 annually. We didn't worry about that, though. We were willing to make some sacrifices, knowing that completing the Ph.D. would give us a better life in the future. As we made do with cheese and crackers, we fantasized about future days when I would be a full professor at an Ivy League university and have a new novel on the *New York Times'* bestseller list. Ah, youth.

Some months after moving to Muncie we found out that our first child was on the way. We were happy and our parents were ecstatic. We knew this would add more of a financial burden to us, but we really didn't mind. I took on a part-time job as a reporter for the *Muncie Star* and earned a little money by covering the night desk in the newsroom and working general news assignments on weekends. We didn't have an extra penny for anything, but it didn't bother us. We had nice neighbors, good friends at our new church, and lots of activities related to my work at the university and the newspaper. We weren't suffering—at least, not then.

A few months after our son was born money became very scarce. We were still paying off the doctor bills when my government schooling benefits suddenly ran out. This put a lot of new pressure on us. I had to start teaching an extra composition class each semester at the university, still keep up with my doctoral studies, and work even more hours at the newspaper. More than once my wife and I looked at each other and said, "If only we had saved some of our money when we were rolling in it—it would have made things so much easier now!"

Whenever we really felt low, we would comfort ourselves by saying that our situation was only temporary and that after graduation in a couple of years we would once again be on Easy Street. Besides, we were sheltered in the arms of our Savior and no real harm could ever come to us. Our faith was in God. He would always provide whatever we needed, right? That's what we had always been taught.

But then in 1978 the bottom fell out of everything.

Earlier that year we had learned that our second baby was on the way. We were told to expect the child to be born in early August. Knowing this, I was able to complete all of my course work toward the doctorate that spring and I found a new job as a public relations executive at Manchester College in the small community of North Manchester, Indiana. Things seemed to be looking up for us.

All I had left to complete was my doctoral dissertation in order to earn the Ph.D. That ordeal was drawing to a close. And even though our second baby would be born in August, the very next month I would have a good-paying job to step into. That seemed like perfect timing.

We found a place to rent in North Manchester, we lined up people to rent our home in Muncie, and we started packing our belongings. We planned to move and start our new life as soon as the baby was born.

But then things went haywire. The baby was due to be born around the first week of August, but by mid-August we were still waiting. Even worse, during the last month before delivery the doctors told us they could barely hear the sound of our baby's heart when they examined my wife. We began to get concerned—very concerned.

Finally, on August 19 I took my wife to the hospital for an induced delivery. After a long and agonizing labor—during which time the doctors told us they no longer thought our baby was alive—our daughter was finally born. Her lungs were full of fluid and her heart was beating at half the normal rate. The doctors worked frantically to clear her lungs. A tube was inserted into the baby's chest and a hand pump was used to force the child to accept and expel air. She was born with a complete heart block and was too weak to breathe on her own. She was rushed by ambulance to Riley's Children's Hospital in Indianapolis and put in the Intensive Care Unit.

Meanwhile, back in Muncie, my wife began to lose a lot of blood. She had suffered from anemia during the pregnancy, but her doctors thought it had been stabilized with iron injections. They were wrong. She was transferred to the Intensive Care Unit and then to an Isolation Unit in Ball Memorial Hospital. Visitors were forbidden and her condition was monitored constantly by nurses and doctors.

All this caught me completely off guard. In my wildest dreams I never imagined that something as traumatic as all this could happen to me and my family. Even my best friend was stunned. The only words of comfort he could think to say were, "Let's be thankful that God saw fit to spare the life of your daughter." Indeed, I was thankful for that, but I couldn't help thinking how much *more* thankful to Him I would have been if my daughter had been born without the medical problems.

In the days that followed, new problems arose. I had some fairly good insurance, but the bills it did not cover began to mount up rapidly: doctors, nurses, lab work, blood transfusions, X-rays, prescriptions, consultations, ambulance service—I was responsible for 20 percent of the cost of each new bill. I was in a panic. I had no money in savings, no investments, and no established credit. In fact, I was still in debt to the university for schooling costs I had charged.

My mother was able to come to Indiana for one week to care for my son while I tried to attend to the needs of my wife and daughter. But when my mother had to return to Michigan, I had no money, no helpers, and no options. In desperation I phoned the pastor of our church and asked him to come by my home. He came immediately and I poured out my woes to him. After checking off my long list of tragedies, I confronted the pastor with the question I had been asking for days: "How could God allow this to happen to me? I'm a good Christian. I'm a born-again believer. I teach Sunday school and direct the youth activities; my wife sings in the choir and works in the nursery. We tithe faithfully. We pray each day. We read our Bible. What is going on here? How could God put me in such a terrible predicament?"

Pastor Warren looked quizzically at me. "I'm sorry? Did you just ask how *God* could have put you into such a predicament? Where did you ever get the idea that it was *God's* fault you don't have enough money to take care of your family properly?"

"Well, you certainly aren't going to blame this mess on me, are you?"

"Who else?" insisted Pastor Warren. "When you decided you were mature enough to take on the responsibilities of caring for a wife and children, that called for special commitment on your part. It seems to me that your priorities were not in order."

"But I've *always* put my family first," I protested.

"Maybe you thought you were doing the right things," said the pastor soothingly, "but your decisions just weren't based on sound knowledge. Look around you. It's obvious to me where you've made several mistakes. You bought a home when all you could really afford right now was an economy apartment. You decided to have two children before you were even out of school and settled into a steady, good-paying job. You spent money on a big car instead of purchasing a compact model and putting the difference in a savings account to earn interest for you. You did everything wrong with your money. And now that your mismanagement has finally caught up with you, you want to lay the blame on God. That's just not fair, Dennis. It's *your* fault, not God's."

I was perplexed. "But...but I was always told that if I had enough faith in God, He would always see me through any crisis."

"That's very true," said the pastor, nodding. "But if you had handled your money in a more efficient way, you wouldn't have had the crisis in the first place. God has given men and women free will. That's a wonderful but precarious gift. It provides you with the freedom to soar to unlimited successes, but it also allows you the leeway to fall flat on your face. You're not a robot that God has preprogrammed to perform in one set way. You are allowed to make decisions, choices, and selections. You can create dreams and fulfill them. But with this freedom comes accountability."

"But now that I've messed things up so bad, what can I do?"

"That's simple," answered the pastor. "Clean up the mess."

"But how? I'm no financial genius."

"Just start doing now what you were not doing before," he explained. "Start with the basics. Get your insurances in order. Start saving money. Reduce your expenses. Pay off your debts. Start studying how money is invested. Begin with the Bible. It has a lot of lessons about money management. Whatever you neglected to pay attention to before in regard to finances, start paying attention to it now."

"Isn't it too late for that?" I asked dubiously.

"Not at all," insisted the pastor. "But the sooner you start, the better off you'll be, both financially and emotionally. Money is important. Don't ever forget that."

He didn't have to worry—I never did forget it. In fact, I learned my lesson so well that my entire life was changed that day. So were my Christian views about stewardship, accountability, free will, and personal responsibility. Within a short amount of time not only was my financial picture strengthened but so was my religious faith.

After my wife and daughter were released from the two hospitals, we made the move to North Manchester. I liked my new job and stayed at it for four years. During that time I put my family on a strict budget. We paid off all our bills. We also began to save money for our future.

Month after month I spent my nights reading books and magazines about money management. My wife and I attended a seminar on family finances at our church. I met with the professors of economics and accounting at the college where I worked and asked them to explain a wide variety of investments to me. I had long talks with my brother Gary, an accountant and financial planner, and asked him to explain technical matters to me about the stock market, the bond market, real estate investing, and banking procedures.

Still haunted by my memories of our disastrous family situation in 1978, I continued to study financial matters until I became a walking reference guide on money management. When insurance agents called on me, I knew more about their policies and products than they did. When I called my brother to pose a theoretical question to him about a tax law, he told me I was more thorough in my research than his graduate school professors had been.

Simultaneously, I spent many hours probing the Scriptures to discover what the Bible had to say about money. There was a lot there, but not much of it had ever been used as sermon material. I decided to change that. I began to talk about financial matters to the students in the adult Sunday school class I was teaching. I discovered that other Christians were as amazed as I had been when they discovered the wide range of things the Bible has to say about money.

Probably the most amazing thing we discovered was that the Bible does not praise poverty, nor does it condemn wealth. Instead, we saw examples of wealthy people who did great things for the cause of Christ. Joseph of Arimathaea provided a new tomb for the body of Jesus. Zacchaeus distributed money to the poor. The parent in the parable of the Prodigal Son gave food, clothes, and a ring to his apologetic son. The wealthy landowner mentioned in Matthew 25 provided work and promotions to deserving employees. Example after example came forth to show that money had as much power to do good as it did to do evil. It was all in how it was handled.

This new understanding came to me at about the same time my own financial circumstances had turned from dire straits to prosperity. I was incredibly grateful to the Lord for teaching me, through the words of Pastor Warren, what my financial position could and should be. It changed my life and my lifestyle greatly for the better.

In recent years my wife and I have been able to establish four scholarship programs at a Christian elementary school, provide monetary support for a missions program, and do a lot of other God-honoring things with our money. Having been redeemed by Christ for many years, we were already enjoying the "good life" in the highest sense of the term. However, being financially independent has also allowed us to enjoy the good aspects of life around us. For that we are truly grateful to the Lord.

In the following chapters I want to distill for you the essence of what I learned about how to become financially comfortable, even very wealthy, and not feel guilty about it. Some of what you read will surprise and perhaps stun you. That's all right. A cold shower does the same thing, but it also wakes you up. And that's what I want to accomplish: a new awakening to your financial potential.

Chapter 2

Ten Shocking Truths About Personal Finance

I want to jump right into some of the meat of this book by sharing ten truths with you about cash. Some of these things may be in direct opposition to many of the concepts you were reared by, but keep in mind that what you've learned in prior years has not made you financially independent. As such, maybe it's time for you to gain some new views of money.

Here then are ten truths worth learning.

1. *Having money is good; not having money is bad.*

Ecclesiastes 10:19 says, "Money answers every thing." Second Thessalonians 3:10 tells us, "If anyone will not work, neither shall he eat."

Nowhere in the Bible can you find passages that state that money is not important. You *can* find verses stressing that there are things more important than money, but nowhere can you find Scriptures which say that money is not important. As my friend Steve Hovda used to say, "The reason Jesus spoke so much about money matters is because money matters!"

Nothing takes the place of money for what money was intended to accomplish. It buys shelter, clothing, food, medical services, transportation, entertainment, furnishings, books, education, good grooming, vacations, music lessons, appliances, and hobby materials.

Not all of these items are necessities, but many certainly are. If a family lacks enough food to provide each member a balanced diet, that is bad. If not enough money is available to rent a home or apartment that is free of vermin, bugs, and other health hazards, that is bad. If an individual does not have a warm coat in winter, that is bad. If a person has an accident and cannot pay for a proper stay in a hospital, that is bad. If a talented young person cannot attend college because funding is not available, that is bad. Each of these bad situations can be corrected by only one thing: money. Having enough of it provides the good things in life; not having enough of it creates situations of pain, heartache, embarrassment, and missed opportunity. Nothing takes the place of money for the specific areas that money was meant to supplement and serve.

I had a dear Christian friend who had served the church and the cause of Christ right up until his death at age 82. He had started as an itinerant minister who pastored three small congregations in southern Indiana for 12 years. Later he was a Bible professor and a dean at a small Christian college. He never made large salaries, so his wife worked full-time during most of their married years. Eventually she retired and her company sent her and her husband on an all-expenses-paid trip to Europe. That trip was the most enjoyable experience either of them ever had. In fact it was the *only* thing of major personal indulgence they had ever allowed themselves. Frankly, they could never afford anything else.

I often asked my friend how he felt about money matters and how he was preparing for his future. His answers always disturbed me, for he would respond with platitudes about how if the Lord could care for the birds of the field, He could also care for His servants. When I pointed out that the Lord provided for the birds of the field, but He didn't throw worms into their nests, my friend would just change the subject.

Six months before his death, this dear saint of God developed stomach cancer. His dying was slow, painful, and very costly. His available cash disappeared amid a stack of doctor and pharmacy bills. He waived the idea of entering a hospital for constant treatment and instead stayed at home. His wife came out of retirement and found a part-time job to help supplement their meager Social Security checks. This separated them during their last few weeks of possible companionship.

Prior to his death my friend called me to his bedside. He told me that he had decided to have his body cremated because it would eliminate the costs of a casket, funeral parlor, tombstone, and gravesite. He knew his widow simply couldn't afford these things. She still had four more years of mortgage payments to make on their home, she was about to lose the income of one of their Social Security checks, and her health was beginning to require a doctor's care, for her legs were weak.

When I asked my friend if he was positive that he wanted to be cremated, he said he was. He added an interesting comment, however. He looked at me and said, "When you are old and sick and you spend day after day lying in bed, you have plenty of time to think about how you would relive your life. I've done that, and I can honestly say I have no regrets except for one. When I failed to save and invest money, I did it because I felt I was always capable of serving the Lord and working to care for myself. I forgot, however, that my stewardship of money also impacted my wife after my death. It grieves me to die penniless and not leave her with enough cash to allow her to enjoy her remaining years."

The man's words were prophetic. After he died, his widow put their home up for sale, cut down on all her living expenses, and found it necessary to go back to work full-time. Our church sees to it that the woman lacks none of the basic necessities of life, but her radical

change in lifestyle was something we were unable to
prevent from happening. Not having money was a bad
situation for this dear lady. It was a situation that could
have been avoided had her husband (or she) begun even
a modest savings program early in their marriage.

The same is true of you. You *need* money. We all do.
Not to accumulate money is both naive and dangerous.
Never forget that fact.

If you follow the plans set forth in this book, you will
acquire enough money to meet your needs and the needs
of those who depend on you. Christians have an obliga-
tion to provide for themselves if they are physically able
to do so. You should not have to be a burden to your
friends, the state, or private charities. Possessing money
is not bad; what's bad is not possessing it when you need
it for appropriate reasons.

2. *Money CAN buy happiness ... and respect and security and contentment.*

Ecclesiastes 7:12 says, "Wisdom is a defense as money
is a defense."

Research conducted by the R & R Newkirk Company
over several decades revealed a success/failure ratio in
groups of men. That ratio did not vary from one era to
the next, no matter how prosperous or lean the economic
times were. It was discovered that if you follow the lives
of 100 men chosen at random from age 25 these results
could be expected at age 65:

1 man will be very wealthy

4 men will be financially independent

5 men will still be working to support themselves

36 men will already have died

54 men will be penniless and unemployed, and
will be dependent on welfare, private charities, relatives, and Social Security checks
for support

Of the men listed above, which group do you think is
happier: the five men at the top who have plenty of
money and are financially free to do whatever they
please, or the 54 men at the bottom who are existing
from one handout to the next?

What we see here is that money can indeed buy some
of the elements that lead to a happy life. Money can also
ease our mind over how to pay the rent or whether to eat
out at a nice restaurant now and then.

Saying that money can in a certain sense buy happiness in no way negates the joy of one's personal salvation,
which cannot be purchased with cash. I accepted Christ
as my Savior when I was seven years old during a vacation Bible school class. Since then I've had a special
happiness that makes me content in all situations because my eternal salvation is secure. But that has not
prevented me from having a rollercoaster financial life.
As a teenager I lived at home for free while I had a
terrific job as a part-time music teacher at a local music
store. I had so much money that I bought myself a new
Mustang automobile, filled my closet with new clothes,
and even took a trip to France, Belgium, and Germany.
Later, as a college student and then as a newlywed, I
hardly had one penny to rub against another. Times
were so lean that I couldn't even afford a daily newspaper. Today, as the author of a couple of dozen books,
I've got everything I need... and then some.

Looking back on it all, I can say truthfully that I've
always been a redeemed child of God and a happy Christian. However, I have truly been my happiest when I've
had money in the bank instead of unpaid bills stacked

on the kitchen counter. Anyone who says that money cannot buy happiness is either a person who has never had any money or a person who is afraid to go out and discover all the happiness there is in this great world around us.

If we can agree that money can provide many basic elements of happiness, why is it that only 5 people in 100 ever accumulate any substantial amounts of money? It is because *most people don't understand the basic principles of how money can be earned, saved, and invested.*

Here's one quick example: The modern workweek was certainly not designed to make people wealthy. Each calendar week has 168 hours, but each *workweek* is only 40 hours long. It stands to reason that if you work for 40 hours earning money, but spend the remaining 128 hours consuming the money you have earned, you will be using up money three times faster than you will be earning it! It's a losing battle.

During 40 hours each week you may be earning from 5 to 50 dollars per hour, depending on your career or occupation. The minute you leave work, however, you quickly start expending that cash. You drive home in a car that you're making payments on; it burns expensive gas and oil; it wears out its tires and mechanical parts as you drive; and it requires expensive insurance coverage. Then you arrive at the house that you're still making mortgage payments on. You walk in and turn on the lights and the air conditioning or heating, thereby increasing your utility bill. You open a high-priced can of dog food for your pet and then get yourself a drink. Your refrigerator, burglar alarm, electric clock, and 20 other appliances have been running all day and night, thereby increasing your utility bills nonstop. Your phone service is being charged to you 24 hours per day, with extra costs for all long-distance calls. As you open the mail you find bills for your credit cards, your city/county/

state/federal taxes, your children's school tuition, the dentist and doctor, seven magazine subscriptions, the cable TV hookup, last summer's vacation, and your new Christmas club at the local bank.

You realize that you're on a treadmill: For every dollar you earn, you're spending four. To keep up, you charge more, borrow more, go deeper in debt, and never seem to get ahead.

Clearly, no one gets rich by working a straight 40-hour workweek. It's a matter of simple mathematics. Invest more time in spending than you do in earning and you're going to go broke.

But for the sake of counterpoint, let's examine the other extreme. Let's suppose that you work *two* 40-hour workweeks during each 168-hour calendar week. This means that you're working 80 hours and have 48 hours left for yourself. Now you've reversed the negative-cash-flow situation, since you're earning money twice as fast as you're spending it. At this rate you'll become rich— providing, or course, that your health holds out and that you're working at a job that pays a steady, dependable, reasonable salary. Understanding one basic lesson such as this can go a long way in helping you to get out of debt and on your way to wealth.

Money can indeed buy happiness, but it takes extra effort to earn extra money. If you want the happiness, you'll have to have the money; if you want the money, you'll have to put out the extra effort. This seems like a very simple principle, but for many people it never becomes obvious. And that's why they aren't happy.

3. *The rich do get richer and the poor do get poorer.*

Deuteronomy 15:11 says, "The poor will never cease from the land."

Have you ever stopped to count all the bromides,

clichés, and adages that bring out the point that the more money you have, the more money you'll get? You've heard them: "It takes money to get money"; "The bigger the deal, the bigger the payoff"; "Money begets money, and more money begets more money."

Such lines have remained with us for a good reason: Money increases at a ratio that defies ordinary thinking. The sooner you understand this, the sooner you will become wealthy.

Let me make it simple. Consider the law of gravity. If two objects are dropped at the same time from the same height, they will hit the ground at the same time. Weight has no relationship to acceleration. If you release a one-pound ball and a ten-pound ball at the same time, they will hit the ground at the same time. Galileo discovered this principle hundreds of years ago when he dropped two objects from the Leaning Tower of Pisa.

This law does not hold true with money, however. In fact, the reverse is true. With money, the greater the amount, the greater the acceleration. Let me prove it by showing you an easy illustration.

Two men were challenged to raise $50,000 as quickly as they could. One man was given $1 and was instructed to increase its value to $50,001. Once he accomplished this, he was supposed to return the $1 of seed money but he was told he could keep the remaining $50,000. The second man was given $50,001 and was instructed to raise it to $100,001. Upon accomplishing this, he would have to return the $50,001 of seed money, but he could keep the remaining $50,000.

Neither of these two men knew anything about how to invest money. As a result, they put their money into passbook savings accounts at a local bank that was paying 5 percent interest. After four years they asked to see how much interest their accounts had earned. Here is what they were shown.

Date	Man A	Man B
First Day	$1.00	$50,001.00
Year 1	$1.05	$52,501.05
Year 2	$1.10	$55,126.10
Year 3	$1.16	$57,882.40
Year 4	$1.22	$60,776.53
Total Earnings	$ .22	$10,775.53

The differing results were staggering. Both men had been given the same challenge: to raise $50,000 of new money. Nevertheless, the earning power of the second man's money was immensely greater than that of the first man. After four years of being deprived of the use of his dollar, the first man had 22 cents profit to show for his effort. Or so he thought. At an average annual rate of inflation of 6 percent, the man would actually have *lost* buying power for his original dollar. (The poor just become poorer.)

The lesson here is that you need to have a disciplined saving and investing program, because until you increase your base capital to a significant amount, you'll never enjoy the profits of accelerated earnings. Said in a more direct way, if you want to be richer, you first have to be somewhat rich.

4. *Compound interest is the eighth wonder of the world.*

Matthew 25:27 says, "You ought to have deposited my money with the bankers, and at my coming I would have received back my own with interest."

I was visiting recently with a young couple who had just purchased a home. I complimented them on its design and layout, and they chatted eagerly about what plans they had for decorating the various rooms. During our conversation the wife said, "We only paid $30,000 for this house and it's very nice, but one day we hope to own one of the $75,000 to $90,000 homes here in our neighborhood."

"You already do," I said with a slight grin. The wife looked puzzled, so I went on to explain, "If you multiply your monthly payment times 12 months, that will give you the amount you are paying the bank each year for this house. If you then multiply that amount times the 25-year length of your mortgage, you will discover that you are paying about $80,000 for this home."

The woman stared at me as if I had grown another nose. "That can't be true," she said at last. "We simply can't afford an $80,000 home." She went to a nearby desk and picked up a pocket calculator and began to multiply the numbers I had mentioned. After half a minute she looked at her husband with a pale face and said with a gulping voice, "He's . . . he's right, Fred. If we stay here the full 25 years we're going to pay more than 80 grand for this little house." (And with that they asked me to leave. I now know what *not* to say at a housewarming party!)

That dear couple learned why the tallest buildings in any town are owned by the banks and insurance companies: When you have compounded interest working for you, you become very wealthy. That same couple also learned why they might never own a home better than the one they were currently living in. When you have compounded interest working against you, you throw most of your money down a hole.

It boggles the mind to consider how wealthy a person can become when he or she will put compound interest to work for his or her future. If Columbus had put $1 into a passbook savings account earning 5 percent simple interest in 1492 when he came to America, today his account would be worth approximately 25 dollars. However, if he had put $1 into a passbook savings account that was paying 5 percent *compounded* interest, today his account would be worth more than 39 billion dollars!

I don't know about you, but I consider that a sizable difference!

Most financial counselors realize that teaching people the value of compound interest is one of the best ways to get them on the road to financial recovery. Therefore, even when people are desperately deep in debt, the counselor will make them start saving 10 percent of their monthly earnings. This 10 percent is usually put into a money market fund or a mutual fund so that it can earn a high rate of interest. A year or two later, when the persons being counseled have finally brought their debts under control, they also have a savings fund. The counselor then shows them that they have invested a certain amount of money, yet what they now have in their fund is much higher than what they've saved because every 90 days (or sooner) the compound interest was added to their total. As time passed, the interest also earned interest, and the new earnings kept increasing faster and faster. What had previously worked to nearly bankrupt them was now working to make them financially independent. That makes these people very happy.

The same rules apply to you. If you buy things on your credit card and pay 19 to 21 percent interest on the borrowed money, you are making other people rich. If you wait and pay cash for your purchases and invest the difference in an interest-bearing account, you'll be making *yourself* rich. Ben Franklin said, "A penny saved is a penny earned," but today every penny saved at compound interest can mean a *nickel* earned! That's progress that you can literally take to the bank!

5. *If you want to make money, seek the advice of people who have already made money.*

Proverbs 21:20 says, "There is a desirable treasure, and oil in the dwelling of the wise, but a foolish man squanders it."

If you were going to make a wedding cake, would you call up a landscaper and ask for advice? No way. So why is it that people accept investment advice from their barbers, their cousins, their neighbors, and their bridge club members, even though these people have had no meaningful experience in investing? Simply put, it's because everybody hopes to make a pile of money someday by getting in on the inside track of some amazing deal...and they just never know when or from where that chance may arise.

How absurd! Just last week a man at one of my workshops told me, "I have it on good authority that you should buy as much XYZ stock as you can get your hands on. It's really going to climb in value." When I asked the man who his "good authority" was for this information, he answered, "My boss let me in on it and he heard it from some guy he knows who is really sharp in investments." I passed. The recommendation of "some guy" doesn't hold much weight with me.

I discovered long ago that people who know how to make money also know how to explain to others how it is done. My brother Gary is very good at this. He holds an MBA degree and he is a licensed broker and a registered accountant. Years ago I asked him if I should take $9000 out of my bank savings account and invest it in stocks. He said yes and he then told me why. He began by pointing out that my $9000 was earning 5.25 percent interest for me, which was a total of $472.50 per year. Stocks, he explained, could earn much more.

He showed me a stock that was selling for $18 per share and told me I could buy 500 shares of it for my $9000. This stock was paying a 14 percent annual dividend, which meant that my earnings would be $1260 per year. This pleased me very much, but the best was yet to come.

He then explained that if I sold five "covered call" contracts on my stock, I could earn a bonus of $250 every

90 days. This was true because people were willing to pay me 50 cents for each one of my shares of stock as a guarantee from me that if the stock rose in value from $18 to $20 I would sell my 500 shares to them at the $20 price. If the stock did not rise in value, I could just keep the $250. This added another $1000 of annual earnings income to my stock and made the total annual return equal to 25.11 percent interest. Wow!

At the end of that year my stock did rise to $20 per share and the person with the option on it bought it from me. So here's what happened: I invested $9000. It earned 14 percent dividend for $1260 that year. It earned $1000 in covered call sales. It rose $2 per share in value for yet another $1000 in earnings. The grand total return on investment was $3260. That gave me a 36.22 percent interest rate. Double wow!

My brother then reminded me that since I had already incorporated myself as a business, I could buy stocks in the corporate name. I asked him why I should consider that. He explained that when one American corporation buys stock in another American corporation, the dividends are 80 percent tax free as an incentive to keep investment dollars within our own country. I smiled broadly at that news. The next time out I bought the stocks in the name of my corporation. The profits were equally as good, but now only 20 percent of the earnings could be taxed. Triple wow!

The point here is that if you really want to make money, you should get advice from people who have studied money management and proved their knowledge of its mastery by earning a lot of money for themselves. Let *real* money talk.

6. *You CAN get something for nothing ... if you learn about investments!*

Proverbs 23:23 says, "Buy the truth, and do not sell it, also wisdom and instruction and understanding."

If you spend any amount of time reading books about investments and cash flow management and leveraged buying, you will frequently come across the acronym OPM. This stands for "Other People's Money," and it can refer to anything from an advance on your allowance to a major loan from a bank. Basically, it just means that you have borrowed cash from another person (or institution) so that you can invest it in something you feel will earn you a greater profit than what it is costing you to borrow the money.

When you are successful at this, you end up making a profit on investment money that wasn't yours to begin with. You are getting something for nothing. Let's follow a common instance of how this is done.

Let's suppose you own $5000 worth of stock. Using this as collateral, you can borrow $3000 from your broker at a cost of around 10 percent interest (a cost to you of $331.44 per year). If you invest the $3000 in 20 shares of a stock that costs $15 per share and is paying an annual dividend of 14 percent, you will earn $420 per year. By selling covered call contracts at 25 cents per share of stock every 90 days, you can earn $200 more each year. Thus you will earn $620 each year in dividends and covered call sales and you will pay $331.44 per year in interest. You wind up with a profit of $288.56 and it wasn't even your extra $3000 to begin with. What's more, some of the interest you had to pay will be tax deductible and that will increase your profit even more. The broker gets a profit, you get a profit, and the company you invested in gets the use of your money to expand its operations. It's a win-win-win situation, and best of all it cost you absolutely nothing!

Naturally, there is always the risk of buying into a stock (or other investment) that will not reward you adequately to justify the cost of your loan. To avoid this, refer to point 5 above and get the right kind of advice before you borrow the cash.

Wise investors are always on the lookout for something for nothing. You were told before that there was no such thing. Now you know that isn't true. For the shrewd investor, there are a lot of free lunches.

7. *Using leverage tilts everything in your favor.*

Mark 12:43 says, "This poor widow has put in more than all those who have given to the treasury."

The Bible is filled with examples of something small outweighing something large. The compensation factor that makes the two entities become equal or even become tilted in favor of the smaller entity is *leverage*. Gideon only had 300 men to fight alongside him; however, each was a handpicked expert at combat. Furthermore, Gideon and his troops were working with a flawless battle plan. This gave them the leverage they needed to defeat their larger-numbered foe.

Leverage is not hard to understand. If a huge boulder is too heavy for you to move, you can roll a fulcrum log next to it and then pry the boulder loose by inserting a wedging stick between the log and the boulder. When you push your weight down on the end of the stick, it acts as a lever to lift the boulder.

Financial leverage works the same way. A small amount of cash positioned correctly can raise greater amounts of cash. Just as your weight was magnified when you pressed down on the lever to move the boulder, so too can the weight of your money be magnified when it is wedged between two investments and used to leverage one against the other.

Let's look at two examples of how this works.

"Shared loans" make it possible for a small amount of money to earn interest in two places simultaneously. If you have a passbook savings account at a bank (or a savings and loan company), you are probably earning somewhere around 5 percent compounded quarterly interest on your money. If you have $1000 in the account this means you are earning $50.95 each year.

You can go to the same bank or S&L and "freeze" your account (your passbook is taken back from you and you cannot withdraw your money from your account). Once your account is frozen, this becomes guaranteed safe money for the institution. As such, you can use it as collateral. Your money continues to earn 5 percent compounded interest for you, but you cannot withdraw any of it until the frozen account is activated ("thawed") again.

With your account as collateral, you can borrow $900 from that same bank or S&L. Because the loan is secured by your account, you will be given a lower-than-average interest rate on your loan. Let's assume it is 9 percent. This means you will have to pay $83.77 per year for the money you have borrowed. Now you have a "new" $900 to invest. Let's suppose you decided to put this into a corporate bond that will earn 12 percent annual interest. This gives you new earnings of $112.95 per year.

Your summary portfolio now looks like this: $50.95 + $112.95 corporate bond earnings = $163.90. When you deduct the $83.77 loan fee, you wind up with $80.13 remaining profit. This equals an 8 percent return on investment, and that's an extra $29.18 you would not have earned if you had left your money in the regular passbook savings account at 5 percent ($50.95). Your little bit of money worked as a lever to lift your earnings to higher levels.

Once you eventually pay off your $900 loan, you will still own the $900 corporate bond. You can either activate your savings account and reclaim your money or you can let it go on earning 5 percent interest and use it again as collateral to borrow another $900. If you decide to use it for a second loan, you can buy another corporate bond. Then you will be paying out 9 percent on $900, but you will be earning 12 percent on $1800 and 5 percent on $1000. As you can see, this can get to be great fun after awhile. And it's not the only way to use financial leverage.

Insurance loans are another way to leverage your money. If you have a whole life insurance policy, you can probably borrow money from it at a mere 5 percent interest rate (perhaps even less). Let's suppose you decide to borrow $375 for 21 years. This would require $689.67 to repay the loan. If you applied the borrowed $375 against the principal owed on your 11 percent house mortgage, you would reduce your overall house payments over 21 years by a whopping $2055.80. Even after deducting the repayment cost of the insurance policy loan, you would still save $1366.13 (money you would not have to give to the bank in mortgage payments). Thanks to leveraging, your borrowed $375 had a total worth of nearly four times its face amount. Terrific, isn't it?

As we discuss money in other chapters of this book, you will learn other ways to leverage your money. For now, however, be encouraged by the knowledge that even if you don't have a lot of money to start with, you can still earn a lot once you learn how it's done.

8. *Money earned passively spends just as well as income derived from hard labor.*

Psalm 144:13 says, "...that our sheep may bring forth thousands and ten thousands."

Passive income is money you earn from investment vehicles that are in place and earning money for you 24 hours a day. They do not require any active labor on your part. For example, if you have a passbook savings account paying you 5.25 percent interest, you do not have to work for the bank each day to earn that interest; your money earns the interest for you. Your part is passive, not active. But earned passively or not, the interest is still your money. So, knowing this, you soon realize that the more investment vehicles you can get in place to earn passive income for you, the more money you will make and the less work you'll have to do. That's a lifestyle change most folks don't have too much trouble adjusting to.

My best investment in passive income came about when I moved from Muncie to North Manchester to accept the job at Manchester College I mentioned in the previous chapter. My new job provided a college-owned house for me and my family to live in as one of the "perks" for accepting the position. Hearing about this, my father suggested that I should keep my house in Muncie and make it a rental property. I decided to give it a try. My house payment was $125 per month back then, so I put an ad in the paper offering to rent my home for $200, with the renters being responsible for payments of their own utilities. The same day the ad came out a man dropped by and rented it for himself and his wife. They stayed there for two years and paid me $4800 in rent. My mortgage payments totaled only $3000 during that time, so I made a profit of $1800. What's more, I was able to claim depreciation deductions for the house against my taxes because it was now classified as a "business building." On paper it looked as if I was losing money by being a landlord, but in reality I was making a great profit while someone else was paying off my house and I was getting great tax credits to boot. It was so good, I could hardly believe it was legal. (But it was!)

By putting all my rental profits directly against the principal owed on the Muncie property, I paid it off many years ahead of schedule. This saved me thousands of dollars in interest payments. In the interim, my house's $18,000 value had increased to $30,000. So after it was completely paid off I formed a partnership with two friends of mine at my church. My wife and I sold the home for $30,000 to the partnership. We used $4500 to buy into the partnership and kept the remaining $25,500 for ourselves. Now, with "new" owners for the home, we rented it out again and the partnership started the depreciation credits all over again. Today I am still part owner of the property I sold, I am still getting tax breaks from it as a landlord, and once more the renters are paying off my property for me (and my new partners). Amazing as it may seem, it is perfectly legal, totally moral, and wonderfully profitable.

How hard did you work the last time you earned $25,500? Probably a lot harder than I did in earning the money from that house deal, right? Well, my passive earnings spent just as well as your hard-earned cash did. That's why I want you to learn how it's done. In the coming chapters of this book we'll discover other methods of developing passive-income sources.

9. *Money is power.*

Proverbs 22:7 says, "The rich rules over the poor, and the borrower is servant to the lender."

Bankers have their own version of the Golden Rule. It goes like this: "The guy with the gold rules." If you want to have control over your life, you have to possess some of the gold.

When I moved from North Manchester to Fort Wayne in 1982 in order to become a full-time freelance writer, my wife found a nice tri-level home she wanted us to buy. I saw it and liked it too, so we made an appointment with a realtor to go to the bank and set up a mortgage purchase for it.

When we sat down with the loan executive to arrange the paperwork, he asked what I did for a living. When he heard I was a writer, he said, "You mean you have no steady form of income, yet you expect us to loan you enough money to purchase this house? I'm sorry, sir, but that's out of the question."

I went on to explain that my writing career was very secure. I assured him he wouldn't have to worry about my ability to meet the payments. I even showed him my signed contracts for new books. He still looked skeptical. This began to annoy me.

"If you're a successful writer, why haven't I ever heard of you?" insisted the loan officer.

"I don't know," I said, growing irritated. "Can you read?"

At this point my wife reached over and touched my arm as a signal for me to calm down.

"How much would a down payment for this home run?" my wife asked.

The banker mentioned a figure to my wife. She reached into her purse, took out her checkbook, wrote a check for that amount, and handed it to the man. She then handed him a copy of the paid mortgage on the home we already owned in Muncie and suggested that it be used as collateral for the new home.

The banker's mouth fell open in surprise. It took him a moment to recover from his shock, but once he did he was instantly all smiles. He raced through the paperwork, gave us a free calendar and pen with the bank's logo on them, handed us each his business card, and asked us to call him personally if we ever had any other banking needs.

The moral of the story is this: Nobody laughs at people with money.

10. *You cannot increase cash flow by reducing overhead.*

Ecclesiastes 5:4 says, "Pay what you have vowed." First Thessalonians 4:11,12 says, "Mind your own business... work with your own hands... that you may lack nothing."

One serious mistake that many people make is in

misunderstanding what literal cash is and what figurative cash is. For example, reducing your overhead expenses makes your existing money (literal cash) stretch further, but it does not generate new cash in your hands. Figuratively speaking, there is "more" money, but in reality there is no physical cash actually to hold. If you move from a $500-per-month apartment to a $400-per-month apartment your expenses have been reduced by $1200 per year, and that's good; however, if you suddenly need some money to repair your car or to buy a new dress or to pay some back taxes, you do not actually have an extra $1200 to spend. People often make the mistake of using their credit cards to spend "ghost" money. This only puts them deeper in debt and increases their money problems. A year later they are forced to move into a $300-per-month apartment and they are baffled over their continued decline in prosperity.

For this reason we will spend equal amounts of time in this book learning how to reduce overhead (live within a reasonable budget) *and* how to generate new income. To succeed as a money manager, you need to know how both are accomplished.

You have now been confronted with ideas that may seem radical to your normal way of thinking about money, but on the other hand, I'm sure you've also been captivated by these ideas. That's good; keep an open mind, because there's a lot more ahead for you to learn.

Chapter 3

Money:
Hard Come, Easy Go

In early 1989 I entered the faculty lounge at the Fort Wayne extension campus of Indiana University, where I teach as an adjunct faculty member. An argument was already well under way. Five faculty members were debating the new salary schedule that had been released by the college chancellor.

"I guess it's the best we could hope for," one woman lamented.

"Are you kidding?" a teacher next to her retorted. "These raises are insulting. Why, if I were in industry I would be making three times this much."

"Maybe," said an older woman, "but you wouldn't have the protection of tenure. At least here you can't get fired on the spot for one small mistake."

"But Sue is right," a man near the coffeepot chimed in. "There are people in other lines of work who have none of the educational training we have, yet they're making far more than our salaries. That's not right. It just isn't fair."

"I agree," said another teacher. "It's ridiculous. Why should some 23-year-old baseball player who can't even sign his name be paid $250,000 each summer when I'm here with a Ph.D. in French and I'm only earning $31,000 a year? I mean, the rule that people live by is, 'You get paid what you're worth.' Isn't that right?"

"No," I said flatly, not waiting to be asked my opinion. All eyes turned to me.

"What do you mean 'no'?" they asked.

"You don't get paid what you're worth," I explained. "You get paid what you're worth *to other people.*"

"What's the difference?" someone challenged.

I smiled. "There's a lot of difference. Dr. Jenson here has a Ph.D. in modern languages and he teaches four classes of French. Each class has about 20 students in it. So on any given day he is of value to about 80 people. In fact, for 15 consecutive weeks—one semester—he is of value to *only 80 people.* However, when Jose Conseco hits a home run out of the ballpark, or Larry Bird slam dunks a game-winning basket, or Mike Tyson knocks out his opponent in the fifth round, they please crowds of thousands of people—in fact, hundreds of thousands of people if you consider TV coverage. Now in fairness, who should be paid more, the person who is of value to 80 people or the person who is of value to 800,000 people?"

"But what about the *value of knowledge*?" someone argued. "Surely that should be worth more than a short season of athletic entertainment."

"But what is the value of that knowledge *to other people*?" I insisted. "A person's worth will always be determined in accordance to what value he or she is *to other people.* When Henry Kravis, one of the partners in the investment management firm of Kohlberg, Kravis and Roberts, arranged for $4 billion to be borrowed by Donald Kelly so that he and his associates could buy Beatrice Foods, Mr. Kravis earned fees and commissions of $400 million in 16 months. Now *that*, my friends, is what I call selling your knowledge for the right price! The point was, Kravis knew how to raise the needed loans, so he was paid in accordance to the *value of his knowledge.*"

"Are you implying that what I teach is of lesser value than what other people provide in their careers?" Dr. Jenson demanded of me.

"Not at all," I said. "It's of equal value, but not to as many people. And that's the difference. Financial compensation comes down to this: The more people you please with what you do and the limits you will go to in order to please those people will determine what you get paid."

"So where does that leave *us*?" asked one of the professors.

"In the middle," I answered. "You can either stay at what you're doing and learn to be content, or else you can opt to enter a different profession in which you can be of more value to greater numbers of people."

And with that they all filed out of the lounge with frowns on their faces.

Financial Facts of Life

As you can imagine, I didn't win any popularity contests with those professors. Like the kings of ancient days who killed the runner who came back from the battlefield with news of a lost battle, these teachers wanted to kill me for speaking the undesired truth. But not facing up to the truth could no more change the truth today in relation to finances than it could change it in ancient times in regard to lost battles. Facts are facts.

What depresses most people is that they don't have the athletic skill of a Larry Bird or the management acumen of a Henry Kravis. Knowing this, they become convinced that there will never be a chance for them to make the "big kill" financially. And they're right. In fact, very few of you reading this book will ever have someone offer you a million dollars for your services.

So, if we can't get rich quickly, yet we still want to get rich, how do we go about it? The answer is to get rich slowly. It takes us awhile longer, but we still achieve the same objective. Here's how it's done.

The first step is to create a financial profile of yourself. You do this in two ways: 1) by calculating how much you are worth financially and 2) by discovering what your tolerance for risk is in taking steps to increase your wealth.

The table on the next page (Figure 1) is for you to use in tallying your current net worth. Take time out now to work out these calculations. Once you have subtracted the liabilities from the assets, you'll have a clear indication of how prosperous you have been so far in your life. In the next chapter we will show you ways in which to increase that amount.

Discovering Your Tolerance for Risk

In order to increase your assets and personal wealth you are going to have to take some investment risks. People have spent their lives looking for "risk-free" investments, only to find that none exist. During the 1920's people thought their savings accounts were safe, but they lost everything when the bank crash came. Today, people who have bank savings accounts have their money federally insured up to $100,000, yet they still aren't totally safe. If inflation climbs to 14 percent, as it did during the years of the Carter administration, a 5 percent passbook account will actually be losing 9 percent of its buying power.

Gold has been considered the universal currency. Nevertheless, during the 1970's it whipsawed in value from $35 an ounce to $857 an ounce and to all points in between. During the Bunker Hunt attempt to corner the market on silver, the price of silver rose from $3 an ounce to $17 an ounce and then collapsed to $2.80 an ounce. Depending on when you jumped into these markets and got back out again, you could have made a fortune, broken even, or lost your entire grubstake.

DETERMINING NET WORTH
An Inventory of Liabilities and Assets

LIABILITIES—

All Outstanding Debts	Self	Spouse	Combined
Accounts payable (credit card balances, insurance premiums, utilities, tuition, rent, food, other bills)	$	$	$
Loans			
Mortgages			
Taxes			
Charitable pledges			
Other			
TOTAL	$	$	$

ASSETS	Self	Spouse	Combined
Accounts receivable (money owed to you)	$	$	$
Cash in bank (checking and savings accounts/certificates)			
Securities, mutual funds, money market funds			
Other investments			
Keogh, IRA			
Personal property (autos, home furnishings, silver, jewelry, clothing, etc.)			
Residence(s), other real estate			
Annuities			
Cash value of life insurance			
Employee benefits (vested interest in pension & profit-sharing plans, etc.)			
Business interests			
Miscellaneous TOTAL	$	$	$

	Self	Spouse	Combined
TOTAL ASSETS	$_____	$_____	$_____
TOTAL LIABILITIES	$_____	$_____	$_____
NET WORTH (Assets minus liabilities)	$_____	$_____	$_____

Figure 1

Real estate in Texas and Oklahoma during the 1970's doubled, tripled, and quadrupled in value as people left the Rust Belt for the Sun Belt. Then suddenly during the 1980's the OPEC nations flooded the world markets with cheap crude oil and real estate in Texas and Oklahoma (financed by oil money) became virtually worthless.

Examples abound in regard to the upside and downside risk aspects of all investments. The simple fact remains, however, that nothing ventured means nothing gained. Like the turtle, we can make no advancement unless we dare to stick our neck out occasionally. The best way to do this is by knowing what the risks are. Let's review them.

Business risk. Anytime you start a business of your own or invest in someone else's business you run the risk of losing your capital if the business should fail. In order to protect yourself, you should make sure that your company's products are not destined to become obsolete or that its management does not get out of step with competitive new marketing strategies. Read annual reports and keep abreast of the market, its products, and its customers' needs.

Liquidity risk. Whenever you tie up your money for extended periods of time, you run the risk that a crisis might arise in your life which will necessitate the use of that money. With some long-term investments, such as real estate holdings, you might be forced to sell at a time when the market is in a slump, causing you to lose most of your investment. Other long-term investments, such as IRA's, allow you to retrieve your funds, but only after you have paid stiff penalties and fines for early withdrawal. It's best never to make yourself this vulnerable.

Interest-fluctuation risk. The rise and fall of interest rates can make borrowing or investing risky if money is locked in at a fixed rate for long periods of time. In 1958 my parents bought a home with a 30-year mortgage at only 6 percent interest. This later proved to be a fabulous bargain because interest rates rose to twice that much. But in 1982 I bought a home with a 25-year mortgage at 13½ percent interest. When interest rates fell to 9½ percent interest in 1985 I refinanced my home for the lower rate. It cost me $2240 in points, closing costs, and prepayment penalties to convert my mortgage. What was great for my parents was terrible for me.

Financial-swings risk. Even though you may invest your money in seemingly secure investments, markets can swing up or down for a variety of bizarre reasons. Your stock in a blue chip corporation may plunge simply because one market analyst gave it a bad review in a newspaper column. Your investment in a citrus crop in Florida may flop because of unseasonable weather. Your real estate investment in a condominium in Honolulu may drop to half its value just because trendsetters are saying that Hawaii is out and Jamaica is in this season. It's serendipitous. You never know what mood the markets will be in. That's why it pays to use cautious diversity when investing. If one investment is down, another may be up.

Tax-law changes. Sometimes people put great amounts of their money into so-called "guaranteed tax shelters." But they only remain guaranteed so long as Congress decides to maintain the same laws. In 1987 IRA deductibility was reduced except for self-employed people or those with no company pensions. For thousands of Americans this meant an annual loss of a $2000 tax deduction. Laws change frequently, and sometimes in radical ways. It's not wise to plan your future financial security based on yesterday's financial rulings.

What we see is that *there is an element of risk in any plan to advance financially*. You won't always win because no one always does. Donald Trump would tell you that, and so would Larry Burkett and Ron Blue and Henry Block and the late Malcolm Forbes and any other person who is an expert on financial management. But, by the same token, they would also tell you that you should take a certain amount of calculated risks.

In my lifetime I've made a lot of deals and taken a fair number of risks. Like any other investor, I've failed from time to time. But in each instance I've learned something and it has made me wiser the next time around.

In 1973 I was approached by an investment counselor who asked me to buy a $1000 bond to help raise funds to build a Christian college in Owosso, Michigan. He told me that my money would be used for a God-honoring venture and that it would earn a 9 percent interest rate for me. My wife and I were both working full-time back then and had no children to support, so I invested the money without first carefully researching the project. For about two years we were sent nice dividend checks every six months. Then without warning in 1975, the college went into receivership. Primary creditors were paid with available funds and secondary creditors like me were stuck holding worthless bonds. I lost my $1000 because I had invested with my heart instead of with my head.

In 1986 an investment consortium in New York was selling commercial paper (unsecured notes) which paid 14 percent interest. The investment was risky but the return was terrific. I bought $2000 worth of notes in $500 denominations staggered to mature at six-month intervals. I knew going into this investment that there was a big element of risk, so I only invested money I could afford to lose at no risk to my family's welfare. The first $1000 matured on schedule in 1987 and paid me the large interest bonus. Then in 1988 the company had its assets seized because of undercollateralization. After long court battles and property disbursement procedures that lasted well into 1989, I finally received settlement checks for about $685. So I won in a big way at first then lost in a big way in the end. That's simply the way it is in the arena of investing.

My point in explaining all this to you is to let you know that you should not give up if one or two of your investment ventures do not pan out for you. In fact I want you to know that they definitely *won't* all pan out for you. But that will not mean you have failed; it will mean you have learned something new. There is no failure, only feedback. If a baby quit trying to walk just because it fell on its bottom side a time or two, it would never become mobile. But by continuing to venture away from the handrail, it learns to toddle, then walk, and eventually run. The same process applies to you in learning to handle investment risks. Time and practice lead to confidence and capability.

How much Time?

I sometimes have people come up to me after one of my lectures on financial management and say, "Your information would be terrific if I had a lot of money to begin with, but I don't. I can only invest a little at a time. Should I try anyway, or just give up?" Of course my answer is to never give up. Instead, I ask these people to answer a question for me.

"Which of these plans would make you wealthier? Plan One calls for you to put $10,000 all at once into an account that earns 7 percent compounded interest for 15 consecutive years. Plan Two calls for you to put $100 each month for the same 15 years into an account that also earns 7 percent compounded interest. At the end of the 15 years, which account would have more money in it?"

People always answer, "The account that had $10,000

in it right from the first day," but surprisingly, they're wrong. Under Plan One you would have $27,590 after 15 years, while under Plan Two you would have $34,604. Slow and steady ultimately wins the race. (By the way, after 25 years Plan One would have $54,264, but Plan Two would have a whopping $81,000.)

Let's see how steady savings can make a great difference in your life. We'll look at the lives of two fictitious, but representative, American families.

Mike and Louise Thompson have been married for 17 years. They have a boy, 13, and a girl, 11. They live in a four-bedroom home, drive a two-year-old car, have a lot of nice furniture, and dress well. Last year Mike lost his job as a machinist when his employer modernized the factory and replaced the line workers with robots and computers. Mike was unemployed for eight months but then found work as a morning-delivery truck driver for a bread company. His new job pays him $14,000 less per year than his previous job and the benefits package is not as good. This has put the Thompsons under severe financial strain. They held a garage sale and sold most of their sports equipment, tools, spare TV, pool table, and record collection. But it wasn't enough. Their credit cards were canceled, their newspaper and magazine subscriptions were stopped, and their children were dismissed from the private school they attended because of unpaid tuition debts.

One morning Mike and Louise sat in the family room, staring at the stacks of unpaid bills and invoices. They were dumbstruck by the radical reverse of their financial status.

"For 12 years I made a big salary," said Mike. "I got a 7 percent pay raise every year. I even received an annual year-end bonus. So, where's all that money? I can't believe we didn't manage to save a dime of it. If we had put even a few thousand aside we could have made it through the eight months I was unemployed. Now we're going to have to give the house back to the bank. This is incredible—I can't believe it!"

However, next door to the Thompsons lives the Johnson family. Ted Johnson was laid off at the same time Mike was. He was unemployed for six months, but he spent that time learning to be a computer operator. He's now working as an inventory manager for a large chain of appliance stores. His salary is about $10,000 lower than his former job paid, but he has several opportunities to work overtime and he'll be in line for a big promotion after two years. Unlike Mike, Ted did not panic when he lost his job.

When he started his factory job Ted signed up for the payroll savings plan at work. A small portion of his pay was withheld each week and was used to purchase U.S. Savings Bonds. Although the weekly investment was small, by the time Ted was laid off the bonds were worth more than $15,000. That monetary cushion provided Ted with tuition money to enroll in the computer school and to support his family while he was switching careers.

But each time Mike Thompson had received a raise, he had spent it on a VCR, a microwave oven, a snowmobile, or some other consumer item. Ted Johnson, on the other hand, made steady savings a first priority in his life. And in the end that's what made the difference.

The principle is that *today's prosperity does not insure tomorrow's prosperity*. To determine your financial circumstances you must project your thinking and planning *several years into the future*. You must ask yourself serious questions and prepare now for the solutions and the answers to those questions. Begin by considering questions such as these:

1. If your aged parents need nursing home care, who will pay for it?

2. If you or your spouse become disabled, how will you earn a living?

3. If your children want to attend college, how will you pay for it?

4. If you or your spouse die, how will funeral costs be paid and where will the money come from for babysitters, repairs, and other people to do the work of the deceased spouse?

5. If you get fired or laid off, how will you survive while you are seeking a new job?

6. When it comes time for you to retire, how will you support yourself?

As you consider these questions, you will realize that the time to start planning for their solutions is *now*. This will cause you to review the way your *current* financial circumstances can be adjusted so that they will exert a positive influence on your *future* financial circumstances.

Amateur Investors Make Mistakes

All your life you've probably heard the catchphrase "easy come, easy go." But we all know that money *doesn't* come easy. To get it you have to work, save, budget, invest, and plan. Money may go easy, but it comes in hard. For that reason we need to be cautious about how we use it, especially when it comes to creating a personal portfolio of investments. Let's take a moment to review some of the most common errors that amateur investors frequently make.

Mistake number 1: Paying needless commissions. Many people feel that all investment purchases must be made through a broker or banker. This just isn't true. You can save a lot of money if you avoid paying commissions. For example, U.S. Treasury Bills sell in $10,000 amounts for 13-, 26-, or 52-week maturities. You can order them by mail or in person from any of the 37 regional Federal Reserve banks. If your broker does the ordering for you, he will charge you from $25 to $75 as a commission fee. Similarly, if a realtor sells your $85,000 home and charges you a 7 percent commission, that is $5950 directly out of your pocket. However, if you hire a person known as a "closer" to complete the final paperwork, you can sell your house on your own and pay $150 to the closer to handle the paperwork. With the money you save, you can buy some new furniture. So don't be hasty to hire someone to do something you can do yourself.

Mistake number 2: Forgetting to tithe. We read in 2 Corinthians 9:7 that "God loves a cheerful giver." Malachi 3:8,9 asks, "Will a man rob God? Yet you have robbed Me! But you say, 'In what way have we robbed You?' In tithes and offerings. You are cursed with a curse, for you have robbed Me." Since God owns the earth and everything in it, He doesn't need our money. He wants us to show our faith in Him, however, by supporting the ministries of His church. When we are blessed with any quantity of money, it is our responsibility to return an adequate portion of it to the Lord. If we turn our back on Him, how can we expect Him to bless our financial plans and investments?

Mistake number 3: Being guided by outdated information. After the Crash of '29 my grandmother refused to ever put her money in banks again. She stored her money in jars, under her mattress, and between the pages of hardbound books. I explained to her about the FDIC and the FSLIC, but she would not be swayed. As a result, she never earned a nickel of interest on her cash. If you think she was an odd old woman, think again.

After the stock market crash of October 1987, many people sold off their entire stock portfolios and ran around screaming that the sky was falling. For the next two years the analysts kept saying, "This is the time to buy. Prices are unrealistically low. There's no way you can lose at this." But the memory of the 1987 crash made people leery. As a result, it was the prudent investors who did all the buying. In time the market rose again and the cautious investors then came back into the market at the "safe" (very high) prices. Too bad; they missed a golden opportunity to make some substantial profits.

Mistake number 4: Splintering a portfolio. Taking a hit-or-miss approach to assembling a series of investments defuses the momentum of earnings. Some investors, upon hearing a hot stock tip, rush to the phone and order 50 shares. A month later they hear another tip and buy 50 shares of something else. If you question them about their hodgepodge approach to investing, they'll usually respond, "I believe in diversification." The problem is that random purchases of investments provide *too much* diversification. It takes hours of time each month to keep track of each investment, it costs a fortune in broker's fees to keep placing small-lot orders, and it negates the compounding momentum of one large investment. If you want diversification, invest your money in one or two reliable mutual funds. The funds' managers will provide the diversification, but you'll only make *one* simple payment each month or quarter to the fund. Your paperwork will be reduced, your risks will be reduced, your commission costs will be reduced, and your earnings momentum will be increased.

Mistake number 5: Staying cash-conservative. It may seem logical to keep all your money in guaranteed-return investment vehicles, such as a passbook savings account, investment notes, or Treasury bills. After all, your interest rate will be locked in and there will be no chance of the investment going down in value, the way stocks or real estate can. This is a good practice as long as the economy of the country remains stable, as it did during the eight years of the Reagan administration. However, it can be a devastating plan if the economy goes haywire, as it did during the four years of the Carter administration. If, for example, you have your money in a bank CD earning 8 percent interest for the next ten years and inflation shoots up to 15 percent, you'll be losing 7 percent in annual buying power each year.

This is the reason that Continental Bank of Illinois and hundreds of other banks folded during the 1970's and 1980's. They had loaned money at 6 percent to homeowners for 30-year mortgages. When inflation got out of control, the banks had to pay 12 percent for certificates of deposits just to get people to keep their money in the bank. By loaning money at 6 percent and borrowing it at 12 percent, the banks very quickly went bankrupt. The U.S. Government decided to step in and keep the large banks like Continental Illinois afloat, but the smaller banks were either sold or allowed to go broke. Knowing this, it is wise to invest part of your savings in growth stocks, real estate, and other investments that will rise in value with inflation.

Part of your reason for reading this book is to correct bad spending and investing habits you may have developed over a number of years. The above five points may be part of the trouble you are having. As a Christian, however, your biggest mistake of all may be in thinking that it is wrong to spend so much time setting your mind on money matters. Well, if it is wrong for you, then why did so many people in the Bible focus on money?

Consider these situations for a moment. Why do you suppose the apostle Paul thanked the congregation at

Philippi so graciously for the money the people sent him? (See Philippians 4:18.) Because that money enabled him to live and preach, that's why. Why do you think Joseph instructed the Egyptians to store so much grain during the prosperous years? (See Genesis 41:25-49.) Because he knew that the drought was coming and that only the prudent people who prepared for lean times would survive, that's why.

Why did God the Father direct three wise men to deliver gold and other gifts of wealth to the parents of the baby Jesus? Why did Christ curse the tree that failed to bring forth fruit? Why is the Old Testament so explicit in its laws about proper offerings?

We could ask questions similar to these for hours on end, and in each instance we would come back to the fact that God's people need to know the importance of financial management. "Do you see a man who excels in his work? He will stand before kings; he will not stand before unknown men" (Proverbs 22:29). The Bible makes it clear that God gives us a great deal of personal freedom; however, the freedom carries with it equal opportunities to measure up to our responsibilities or slide to our lowest levels of failure.

Discovering that God expects us to be accountable for our actions is one of the most sobering moments in a Christian's personal maturity. It's a hard lesson, and one that some of us have to be taught more than once before it finally sinks in.

Financial accountability is something that all Christians must face, the sooner the better. If you stick your head in the sand and just hope that things will work out all right in the end, you'll discover that "the end" will come a lot sooner than you had anticipated.

Money does come hard and go easy, but it can be used in very beneficial ways for us if we learn how to master it. You've learned a lot already, but there's more coming. Read on and prosper.

Chapter 4

Starting with What You Have and Getting to the Top

A 25-year-old man once told me that he was too poor to save money. He lamented, "I'm in a dead-end job. My gross salary is only two grand a month. I have no chance for a promotion or a raise. I'll be doing this same job until I retire at 65. There's no hope for me to get rich, is there?"

I paused for a moment and then asked, "Do you think a million dollars would help you get ahead in life?"

The man's eyes lit up. "Well, of course! But where am I ever going to get *that* kind of money?"

"You're practically there already," I explained. "If you can earn $2000 per month from age 25 to 64, you will have a gross lifetime income of $960,000. Work until you're 70 and you'll exceed a million dollars."

"What! That can't be true," the man protested. "Me? A million bucks? In my lifetime? Impossible!"

"Not at all," I assured him. "Figure it out."

I gave him a scratch pad and my pocket calculator. He multiplied 12 months per year times $2000 per month and came up with $24,000 annual salary. If he worked from age 25 through 65 that would be 40 years, so 40 times $24,000 was a total of $960,000. The man was absolutely astonished by the discovery.

"Now consider this," I continued. "If you can decide to live on $900,000 during the next 40 years and invest the other $60,000 at reasonable compounding rates, you can have about $300,000 waiting for you when you reach 65. That would be pretty nice, wouldn't it?"

The man grinned from ear to ear. "Nice? It would be fabulous! I'm nowhere near as poor as I thought I was, am I? This is great!"

Most people are so caught up in bad spending habits that it has made them assume they are poorer than they actually are. The truth is that they have a lot of money, but they just aren't handling it correctly. They aren't even doing the most basic things to help improve their cash control and money accumulation. If you are one of these people, take a moment now to learn some easy ways to start earning extra cash.

Simple Ways to Earn More Money

You don't need the financial acumen of a J.P. Morgan in order to take some simple steps toward increasing the amount of interest your money makes for you. Put your toe into the financial waters by trying these simple steps.

1. *Examine your savings account.* Make sure it is insured by the FDIC or the FSLIC, that the interest is compounded daily, and that the interest rate is competitive (5 to 6½ percent). If the bank or S & L that currently holds your savings account does not meet all of these requirements, move your money to a place that does.

2. *Open a money market account.* If you plan to maintain a balance of at least $1000 in a savings account, move it into a money market account instead. Your money is accessible, yet it earns a higher rate of interest.

3. *Buy CD's at staggered maturity dates.* A certificate of deposit (CD) is an interest-paying debt instrument

issued by a bank. If you cash it out before maturity you may have to pay a penalty, but if you keep it to the full maturity (usually six months to five years, your choice) you can have the earnings mailed to you or you can leave them in to compound. If you invested $3000 in CD's of $500 each that matured after 6 months, 1 year, 18 months, 2 years, 30 months, and 3 years, you would receive a bigger and bigger check every six months. This would be a source of steady cash flow and increased earnings. CD's can be purchased at any local bank. Compare rates and invest where you can earn the most.

4. *Purchase government securities.* Your local bank can sell you safe and inexpensive government-issued securities. U.S. Savings Bonds are sold at a half-price discount. For $25 you can purchase a bond that will mature at a value of $50. (You can buy them with your credit card by calling 1-800-US-BONDS.) U.S. Treasury notes pay a guaranteed rate of interest, and earnings are mailed to you every six months. The minimum investment is $1000 for a length of 1 to 10 years. U.S. Treasury bonds mature in 10 to 30 years (minimum investment of $1000). U.S. Treasury bills mature in 13, 26, or 52 weeks and are sold at a discount rate like U.S. Savings Bonds (minimum investment of $10,000).

5. *Buy into a mutual fund.* Mutual funds are organized by investment companies and are sold through stockbrokers and certified financial planners. The investment company will add your money to the money of numerous other investors in order to buy a variety of funds (stocks, bonds, and commodities). You personally do not have to know anything about the stock or bond markets. Whatever all the investments mutually earn results in how much your fund makes as a profit. You are mailed your share of the profit based on how much of your money helped create the pool of cash. If you do

not wish to withdraw your share of the profit, it can automatically be reinvested for you in the same mutual fund. In this way you will control even more of the pool of money. Some funds are called "no-loads," which means you do not have to pay extra money as a commission for your broker or for the fund managers. Since you are starting small, no-loads will be best for you. You can enter some mutual funds for as little as $100.

The above few examples showed you some quick and easy ways to make extra money. Too many people feel they can't do anything to help themselves until they have saved a few thousand dollars to invest. That's not so. A newspaper carrier who buys only one U.S. Savings Bond per month will manage to save $300 each year, and when the bonds are redeemed at maturity they will be worth $600. The point is, you can start investing with whatever amount of money you have available. (See Figure 2 on following page.)

Here are four tips to help you initiate your investing practices.

1. *Explore a variety of investments*. Go to the magazine section of the public library and examine the investment, craft, and money-management magazines. Make a list of several investments that have a track record of increasing in value with time. Choose one that interests you and fits within your investment price range. Read as many books and articles about that investment as you can.

2. *Find mentors to guide you*. In order to enhance your skills and knowledge about your specific investment, seek out people who can teach and coach you. Join clubs in which fellow enthusiasts can offer you their advice and experience. Develop a pen pal correspondence with traders and dealers across the country. Attend seminars, lectures, and trade fairs related to your investment.

TIME DISBURSEMENT OF
PORTFOLIO INVESTMENTS

Short-Term (3 months to 2 years)

    Savings account—enough for 3 months' living expenses

    Money market funds—maintaining a $1000 minimum balance

    Treasury bills—13-, 26-, or 52-week maturities

    Certificates of deposit—invested at staggered maturities

Intermediate-Term (2 to 8 years)

    U.S. Savings Bonds

    Municipal bonds (tax-exempt)

    Unit trusts

    Conservative stocks with good dividends

    Mortgage funds (Ginnie Maes, Freddie Macs, Fannie Maes)

    High-grade bonds (A, AA, AAA)

    Limited partnerships

    Mutual funds

    Fixed annuities

Long-Term (8 to 35 years)

    Single-premium life insurance policies

    Growth stocks and international stocks

    Income-earning real estate

    Rare coins, art, and collectibles

Figure 2

3. *Constantly upgrade your holdings.* Begin to build your portfolio by buying whatever you can afford. Later you can improve your holdings by trading what you have (and a little cash) for better-quality pieces or more valuable investments. Buy extra quantities whenever you find a bargain. Learn how to trade, barter, negotiate, purchase, and sell.

4. *Enjoy your investments.* Keep in mind that investments should be not only profitable but enjoyable. Hang your collection of paintings for people to see. Read the books you've collected. Talk with your children about your stamp collection. Wear your handmade lace shawls. Display your antiques in your den.

How Little Amounts Can Grow

The compounding effect of small amounts of money is often amazing to people. For example, if you can double $1000 on itself just ten times, you will have more than a million dollars. If you start with just one penny and double it on itself for 30 consecutive days, you'll have more than 10 million dollars!

Getting started is usually the hardest part. The longer time you have for your money to be invested, the richer you will become. You cannot find a better time to start your investing than today. Sometimes the results will be breathtaking. Let me tell you a couple of true stories to prove this to you.

In 1985, when interest rates were still in double digits, it was possible to purchase a United States Treasury zero-coupon bonds for as low as $50 per thousand. This meant that if you paid $50 for a treasury zero bond in 1985 and held it for 28 years, it would be worth a redeemable value of $1000. It so happened that my brother, an accountant, was approached for advice from a 19-year-old client who had been in a serious car accident in 1985. She had received $20,000 as a lump-sum settlement for injuries she had sustained. The young woman wanted to invest the entire amount for her security later in life. My brother helped her invest it all in United States Treasury zero-coupon bonds. As a result, at the age of 47 in the year 2013, that woman will be able to redeem her $20,000 investment for *one million dollars*.

In 1987 a 22-year-old man was honorably discharged from the Army. He had saved some money during his enlistment, and so he invested $2000 in a tax-deferred Individual Retirement Account (IRA). Since $2000 is not a fortune, he asked this question of his broker: "If I continue to earn 12 percent interest each year on my initial investment of $2000, how much more should I invest each year after that if I want to retire with a million dollars?" The broker gave a surprising answer: "If you invest $2000 a year in an IRA for only six years, ages 22 to 27, and then never put another penny into your IRA, at age 65 it will be worth $1,348,440 if you continue to earn 12 percent each year. If you invested $2000 each year from ages 22 to 65 at 12 percent, you would retire with $2,421,625, and you wouldn't have to pay any tax on that money until you started to withdraw it. Additionally, you would get a $2000 tax deduction for each year that you made a maximum contribution."

That's breathtaking, isn't it? For a $12,000 investment that man could secure more than $1.3 million in return! Who says you can't still get rich in America?

Some wit has quipped that most Americans are so busy earning a living that they never make any money. Actually, that lament isn't anything new. More than 2500 years ago the Bible noted, "You have sown much, and bring in little; you eat, but do not have enough; you drink, but you are not filled with drink; you clothe yourselves, but no one is warm; and he who earns wages earns wages to put them into a bag with holes" (Haggai 1:6).

As a consumer-oriented people, we understand all too well the concept that our pockets, purses, and wallets have holes in them. We always intend to start saving and investing as soon as we "can afford to," yet that day never seems to arrive. But you *can* save and invest, and you *must* begin today with whatever you have available. The sooner you start, the greater your ultimate profits will be. (See Figure 3.)

RETURN ON INVESTMENTS

Cumulative Wealth Index: Value of $100 invested at the beginning of the period indicated.

Investment Returns from January 1946 to December 1987

Investment of $100	Average Annual Compound Return	Year-End 1987 Cumulative Wealth Index
Consumer prices	4.5%	$ 635
United States Treasury bills	4.7%	$ 688
Corporate bonds	4.7%	$ 688
Common stocks	11.2%	$8368

Investment Returns from January 1970 to December 1987

Investment of $100	Average Annual Compound Return	Year-End 1987 Cumulative Wealth Index
Consumer prices	6.4%	$ 305
United States Treasury bills	7.6%	$ 374
Corporate bonds	9.2%	$ 488
Common stocks	10.3%	$ 584

Figure 3

Laws of Cash Flow

In my seminars I explain to my students that there are six laws of cash flow management which must be adhered to if individuals plan to increase their wealth base. Here they are:

1. *Individuals must be aware of their personal finances.* You cannot say, "I have an accountant who

keeps my books straight" or "My spouse handles my checkbook." What you *don't* know *will* hurt you.

You should know how much your property is worth, what your level of debt is, and how much coverage you have in life, health, disability, home, car, and disaster insurance. You should understand your retirement plan and your current and future budget needs. Don't be in the dark about your personal finances. Ask questions; do some reading; check the numbers; help pay the bills; start keeping good records; examine receipts; talk about raises and deductions and taxes and savings. When it comes to your financial responsibilities, ignorance is not bliss; it is agony.

2. *Individuals must set specific financial goals.* Nothing in the realm of financial success "just happens," nor is it ever obtained at the last minute. If you have a dream of one day owning a home and you take out a 20-year mortgage to make the purchase, your dream has a deadline of 20 years in the future. If you have a dream of earning a college degree and paying back your loans for tuition within two years after graduation, you have a goal with a six-year deadline.

The wonderful thing about setting a goal is that doing so will automatically present the necessary plan for achieving it. For example, if your goal is to retire early at age 60 with $500,000 in the bank, you must work backward from age 60 to the age you are right now to find out how much you need to put into your retirement fund each year in order to accumulate $500,000. If you want to take a $7000 vacation two years from now, you will have to save about $292 per month for the next 24 months.

Goal-setting is especially important if your dreams are somewhat overwhelming. Suppose, for example, that your dream is to get completely out of debt. That abstract statement will lead you to concrete procedures. If getting out of debt is your ultimate dream, you will need to find out what your total debt is (the target goal), where it stems from (bank loans, frivolous spending), and how to control it (cutting up credit cards, learning to ride in carpools). Step-by-step you will close in on your target objective. (See Figures 4, 5, and 6.) Ultimately you will be successful.

I would encourage you to press yourself to a point beyond what you consider your maximum abilities to be. Don't put a ceiling on your potential. People are so afraid of not reaching a challenging goal that they set a small goal for themselves so that they won't feel like failures. And that's too bad. I would much rather nearly achieve a grand goal than actually achieve a minor goal.

3. *Goals must be directed by budgets.* Creating a budget guards you from being blindsided by an unexpected expense or a forgotten bill. It also serves as a tangible reminder that, *no*, you cannot afford to take out another loan or, *yes*, you do need to eat leftover spaghetti tonight rather than eat out at the local restaurant.

Budgets are constricting at first, but after a time they actually provide greater freedom. If your budget calls for you to set aside $10 per month for car maintenance, after a year you won't feel jolted financially if you suddenly need a new water pump or two new front tires or a new set of brakes. The money will be there.

Similarly, budgets can help build your confidence. Suppose you want to start saving money, but all you can afford is a mere ten dollars per week. On the one hand, that is a large amount of money to squeeze out of the total allowance for weekly expenditures; on the other hand, it sure doesn't look like much when you think of how little ten dollars actually buys these days. It almost makes you not even want to try. However, by sticking to the budget for just one year you will have $520. After the first week of the second year you can add another ten dollars. From this total of $530 you can take $525 to the bank and invest it in $1050 of U.S. Savings Bonds. Follow the plan for five years and you will have $5250 in bonds. It will give you a real feeling of security to cast your eyes on a stack of large-denomination bonds all made out in your name.

If you find that after using a budget for two or three months you are somehow still coming up short of cash, put a small notebook in your pocket and make a note of every item you spend money on. What you will discover is that you are doing a lot of unnoticed spending. If you put 50 cents per day into a soda pop machine, plus toss in a dollar or two each week for collections taken at the office, plus buy an occasional newspaper, pack of gum, pen, or magazine, all of this will add up to an invisible five or ten dollars each week. That can lead to 40 or 50 dollars vanishing from your monthly budget. You will either have to stop all extra spending or else revise the distribution amounts in your budget.

Similarly, if the budget makes you feel like a prisoner who is serving a long, drawn-out sentence, keep a chart or graph of your monthly debt-reduction progress. As you see that graph line go down, down, down, drawing closer and closer to the zero debt level, you'll be encouraged to gut it out a while longer. Most people can endure just about anything as long as they know for sure that a definite end to their misery is in sight.

Finally, once you have used your budget to control your spending and eliminate your debt, continue to use it even when good times return. Just as you slowly yet steadily dug yourself out from your burden of debt, you can just as steadily begin to build a portfolio of sound investments and savings. If, for example, your budget allowed you to pay 250 dollars per month against existing debts, that money can now be put into a savings account, U.S. Savings bonds, CD's, stocks, or other securities. In this way your budget will not only keep you out

RECORD OF LIVING EXPENSES

	Amount Paid Monthly	Total Annual Amount
Housing		
Mortgage/rent	————	————
Furnishings	————	————
Property taxes	————	————
Electricity	————	————
Heating	————	————
Water	————	————
Garbage collection	————	————
Telephone	————	————
Yardwork	————	————
Repairs/maintenance	————	————
Remodeling	————	————
Neighborhood association dues	————	————
Food	————	————
Clothing	————	————
Children		
School lunches	————	————
Allowances	————	————
Tuition	————	————
Lessons	————	————
Club dues	————	————
Car pools/bus fares	————	————
TOTAL	════	════
Entertainment/Recreation		
Eating out	————	————
Babysitters	————	————
Periodical subscriptions	————	————
Vacations/holidays	————	————
Clubs	————	————
Hobbies	————	————
TOTAL	════	════

Figure 4

Transportation

License plates	_____	_____
Gas and oil	_____	_____
Maintenance/repairs	_____	_____
Parking	_____	_____
New tires	_____	_____
TOTAL	=======	=======

Medical Expenses

Hospitalization insurance	_____	_____
Physicians	_____	_____
Dentists	_____	_____
Optometrists	_____	_____
Pharmacists	_____	_____
TOTAL	=======	=======

Insurance

Home	_____	_____
Life	_____	_____
Disability	_____	_____
Automobile	_____	_____
TOTAL	=======	=======

Gifts

Graduations	_____	_____
Christmas	_____	_____
Birthdays	_____	_____
Anniversary	_____	_____
Weddings	_____	_____
TOTAL	=======	=======

Miscellaneous

Tithe/offering	_____	_____
Husband miscellaneous	_____	_____
Wife miscellaneous	_____	_____
Cleaning/laundry	_____	_____
Pet care	_____	_____
Beauty/barber	_____	_____
Jewelry	_____	_____
TOTAL	_____	_____

TOTAL LIVING EXPENSES	=======	=======

Figure 4 continued

STRATEGY FOR DEBT REPAYMENT

In the following columns, list all of your current creditors according to those with the highest rates of interest down to those with the lowest rates. Make a commitment to pay a set amount to each creditor each month. List that monthly amount and then list the payoff date (your goal). Send a letter to each of these creditors and explain your intentions. Should you receive any unexpected extra money, apply it to the bill costing you the most in interest.

Creditor	Balance Owed	Interest Rate	Amount Per Month	Payoff Date
1.				
2.				
3.				
4.				
5.				
6.				
7.				
8.				

Figure 5

INCREASING YOUR MARGIN

	Monthly Amount	Annual Amount
1. Reduce living expenses by:		
_____	_____	_____
_____	_____	_____
_____	_____	_____
_____	_____	_____
2. Reduce debt by:		
_____	_____	_____
_____	_____	_____
_____	_____	_____
_____	_____	_____
3. Reduce taxes by:		
_____	_____	_____
_____	_____	_____
_____	_____	_____
_____	_____	_____
4. Restructure investments by:		
_____	_____	_____
_____	_____	_____
_____	_____	_____
_____	_____	_____
Total margin increase:		_____

Figure 6

of debt, but it actually will make it possible for you to pay cash for your future purchases. Now that's progress!

4. *Individuals should develop an investment strategy.* You don't have to be a CPA or CFP in order to understand the basics of investments. You can borrow books, videos, audiocassettes, and magazines that explain about bonds, stocks, real estate, and other investments from your public library. The time you spend studying these books will literally be financially rewarding to you.

There's an old saying that promises "Any plan will work if you will." In general this statement is true, but I should add that the better a plan is, the better it will work for you. So investigate matters, develop a plan, review and refine it regularly, and start enhancing your cash supply.

5. *Individuals must become disciplined financial managers.* To succeed in any field of endeavor a person must have discipline. This is particularly true in the area of financial management. Tightening the financial belt gets tedious and aggravating after a few months. It takes discipline not to grab the checkbook and go out and relieve the boredom by starting to spend again. It takes discipline to save money now for benefits in the future. It takes discipline to make payments on time in order to protect a credit rating.

Perhaps discipline is your hardest area to cope with. If so, you may have to put yourself into a position of *forced* discipline. People go about this many ways. Some people don't have enough discipline to save, so they ask their employer to withdraw money for a payroll savings plan from their check before they ever get it. Some people turn their entire paycheck over to a financial counselor each week, and then he or she pays the person's bills and gives whatever is left back to the individual. Some people have their paychecks mailed directly to their banks; after mortgage and other loan payments are deducted, the remaining balance is deposited into the individual's checking account.

Only through consistency does any financial plan succeed. We cannot achieve consistency without discipline. The discipline can be self-imposed, or it can be imposed on you, but it simply has to be there.

6. *All financial actions should be God-honoring.* If we begin with the premise that God owns everything, then our perspective on financial management will be one that makes us good stewards of whatever God allows us to "tend" temporarily. Our tithes, offerings, and donations should be generous. Our business dealings should be honest. Our use of money should be purposeful rather than wanton. If we do this, we will hear our Lord speak as the person in Matthew 25:21 spoke: "Well done, good and faithful servant. . . . Enter into the joy of your lord."

Finding Cash to Invest

Getting excited about investing and *having the money to do it* are two different things. It may surprise you, however, to discover how many sources of cash are actually available to you.

Let's begin by looking at your home. Many people are "rich on paper" because they live in an expensive home. This doesn't mean they are walking around with pockets full of money, though. Statistics show that most families earning from $30,000 to $50,000 annually have 65 percent of their net worth tied up in their homes. If some of that cash could be accessed through a home equity loan, it could possibly generate bonus earnings for these folks.

Some people fear to apply for a home equity loan because it carries a stigma of "needing a second mortgage." That is outdated thinking. A home equity loan provides a ready pool of cash at reasonable interest rates, and the interest paid on any loan is 100 percent tax-deductible. The success factor in using home equity loans lies in the ultimate goal of improving your financial condition. If you can borrow $5000 from your home equity account at 10 percent tax-deductible interest and invest it in a bond or mutual fund that will earn you 14 percent, you'll make a 4 percent profit on the deal *and* receive tax-deduction credits for the interest you paid.

Here's another idea: If you and your spouse qualify for IRA plans, you can borrow $4000 from your home equity account and put it into long-range zero-coupon bonds in your IRA. It may cost you 8 to 11 percent to borrow the money, but you will receive an immediate $4000 tax deduction, the interest paid on the loan will be tax-deductible, and the zero-coupon bonds will later mature at a value of $40,000 or more—and all that appreciated value will be tax-deferred until after age 59$1/2$ when you start to draw out the money!

When you visit your mortgage holder to discuss a home equity loan, have your questions ready. Ask how much you'll be able to borrow. It will usually be about 80 percent of the currently assessed value of your home. Ask what the total cost of establishing the account or line of credit will be, including appraisal costs, recording fees, points, and application fees. Ask what the cap is on adjustable rate mortgages and find out if balloon payments are scheduled. Also ask what the monthly minimum repayment will be. Usually it will be $50 per month or 5 percent of the loan, whichever is higher.

Another source of cash is whole life (permanent) insurance policies with built-up cash reserves in them. Although, as we'll discuss next, these policies are not the most cash-efficient ways to purchase life insurance, you may own several of them already. If so, you will be able to borrow money against them at interest rates as low as 3 to

8 percent. This money then can be invested in higher-yielding bonds, stocks, or other investment vehicles.

Besides your home and your insurance policies, you may have other ways of generating cash for investments. Can you rent a room now that your children have moved out? Can you sell one of your cars? Can you work in your home (tutoring? sewing? babysitting?)? Can you sell your old class ring and other pieces of gold jewelry you never wear? Sit for a moment with a piece of paper and a pencil and jot down ways to generate cash.

Of course you do not want to leverage yourself so heavily in borrowing or investing that you become vulnerable to unexpected setbacks. To protect yourself against this, let's review your insurance and cash reserve needs.

Being Properly Insured

Until you are wealthy enough to have adequate cash reserves to care for yourself under any circumstances (being "self-insured"), you'll need proper insurance coverage. To determine the minimum you can get by with, ask yourself these questions:

1. How much will Social Security pay my survivors if I die?

2. How much, if any, life insurance is my employer already providing for me?

3. How much will it cost to bury me, probate my estate, pay for existing bills, and provide transition money for my family?

4. How much money can my spouse expect to earn by going to work after my death?

5. Do I want to provide an education fund for my children or leave an inheritance to my grandchildren?

Having answered these questions, then do some simple arithmetic. Add up the total assets (Social Security benefits, face value of life insurance policies, stocks, bonds, IRA's, spouse's future income, etc.) and subtract from that the total amount of expenses (burial costs, education costs, emergency cash, etc.). If the expenses exceed the amount of total assets, that will be the amount you need in additional insurance.

In buying life insurance there are several options for you to consider.

Term insurance is inexpensive coverage (about $1.25 per $1000 of coverage for a 35-year-old) which pays only when the insured dies during the term of the policy. Many family breadwinners will carry $75,000 of term insurance on themselves until their children are raised and gone. It's cheap coverage, yet it provides for adequate cash in case of the unexpected death of the head of the family.

Permanent insurance (also called "cash-value" insurance) is more expensive and provides less coverage. It does force the policyholder to accumulate some buildup reserves in the policy, but not at competitive rates. So for aggressive investors it's best to buy term insurance and invest the money you save by doing this.

There are other forms of insurance worth discussing with your family's insurance agent. Property and Possessions insurance should be able to replace your dwelling and possessions in case of flood, fire, hail, wind, lightning, or theft. Liability insurance will protect you in case you are taken to court and sued for personal liability claim. Personal liability policies run about $175 for a million dollars of annual coverage. Health insurance may be covered by your employer, but you still need to check to see that it offers major-medical coverage for extended illness. Disability insurance can be important because if you are ill for a longer time than your unemployment benefits provide supplemental pay, or if you are totally disabled and never able to return to your job, you'll need a source of private funding.

Consult with your personal financial planner and discuss ways you can provide adequate insurance coverage at the lowest possible costs. Your goal will be to pay out as little as possible, yet not leave yourself vulnerable in any way.

There are also other forms of "insurance" you can initiate. For example, it's wise to have a supply of reserve food on hand. I keep enough freeze-dried meat, vegetables, oatmeal, dried milk, baking powder, pudding, and other foodstuffs stored in my garage loft to feed my family for two months if necessary. I never worry if there's a snowstorm or a truckers' strike. Whenever you see a sale on canned goods, you can stock up and put a few aside for reserves. (Just rotate the reserves from time to time to keep things fresh!)

It's also good to keep a few hundred dollars in cash on hand just in case you can't get to a bank over a holiday weekend or a cash-payment emergency arises.

No matter where you're at financially, you can start working your way up from there. It will take a new way of thinking, a specific plan, a greater knowledge, and a lot of discipline. But if you're determined, you'll make it!

Chapter 5

Being Wealthy Isn't Sinful, Illegal, or Fattening

At this point you are probably really excited about the potential you have to become wealthy. However, if you were reared (as I was) in a conservative church atmosphere where the accumulation of wealth was silently condoned but never openly endorsed, you are still probably having some difficulty believing that it is indeed permissible for you to strive for financial independence. If you should decide to discuss this with a fellow believer, you will no doubt sooner or later have someone quote to you from chapter 12 of the book of Luke.

Luke 12:16-34 has been used as a screen for people of poor monetary stewardship to hide behind for many years. Unfortunately, if these people would ever really take the time to read and study this passage of Scripture, they would realize that what Jesus was emphasizing was not the merits of poverty, but rather the necessity to keep things in their proper order. His message stressed the point that the salvation of our souls is more valuable than any other commodity, and until that is secured, all other accumulations are meaningless.

Sometimes people get confused, and reverse the priorities of their lives. I've known people who have said, "I plan to become involved in the church one of these days, but right now I'm too pressed for time. I need to go to college, land a good job, work my way up the corporate ladder, buy a big home, furnish it in contemporary style, build up a fat bank account, and then secure my retirement funds. After all that, I'll have some time to serve the Lord."

Christ called this the logic of a fool (verse 20). Men and women should become "rich toward God" (verse 21) before they go out seeking other riches. In His parable, Jesus told of a wealthy man who worried more about how to increase his profit margin than he did about laying up treasures in heaven. It was a fatal mistake, for the man died early in his life and his soul was brought before the judgment seat, where his money could not help him.

After John D. Rockefeller died, someone said to his accountant, "That old guy must have been worth millions. Just how much did he finally leave behind?" The accountant grinned mirthlessly and responded, "All of it."

This was the very same lesson Christ was teaching when he warned, "Take heed and beware of covetousness, for one's life does not consist in the abundance of the things he possesses" (verse 15). The Bible tells us, "It is appointed for men to die once, but after this the judgment" (Hebrews 9:27). No amount of money or possessions can buy your way into heaven. The first step toward obtaining eternal wealth—"a treasure in the heavens that does not fail, where no thief approaches nor moth destroys" (Luke 12:33)—is to accept Jesus Christ as your personal Savior and to live each day under His grace and by His teachings.

Christ had no objection to people working hard for the material things of life: clothes, food, shelter. As He explained, "Your heavenly Father knows that you need all these things; but seek first the kingdom of God and His righteousness, and all these things shall be added to you" (Matthew 6:32,33).

The point is that a person can be rich in God but financially penniless, and conversely that a person can be a financial billionaire but a spiritual pauper. It's all a matter of priorities: *God must come first.* After establishing that fact, the way is made clear to seek the other good things of life without losing perspective of God's plan for us.

THOUGHT PROVOKERS

There are people who will tell you that money is not important to them. I feel that people who say that are the kind of folks who would probably lie about other things, too.

—Zig Ziglar

Money is the sixth sense without which you cannot make a complete use of the other five.

—William Somerset Maugham

There are few ways in which a man can be more innocently employed than in getting money.

—Samuel Johnson

Work spares us from three evils: boredom, vice, and need.

—Voltaire

Every time history repeats itself, the price goes up.

—Douglas R. Casey

If you wait too long, by the time you reexamine your actions and are able to recognize your errors and the opportunities you missed, it is usually too late to do anything about them.

—Dr. David S. Viscott

Another Look at Luke 12

When Christ sent His disciples into distant lands to carry His message, He told them, "Do not worry about your life, what you will eat; nor about the body, what you will put on" (Luke 12:22). There are people today who are convinced that this verse applies to all people for all times. As such, they don't bother to hold steady jobs, adhere to a family budget, or invest their earnings. They feel that this Bible verse has promised them that God will guarantee that they have enough food to eat and enough clothes to wear. But nothing could be farther from the truth: *That verse applied to the first disciples* (compare Luke 22:35-38). Other interpretations are not only incorrect, but dangerous.

On January 5, 1989, an unemployed truck driver named Larry Cottam and his wife, Leona, were arrested for murder in Wilkes-Barre, Pennsylvania. They were held in the Luzerne County Prison without bail. The murder victim in this crime was Eric Cottam, the couple's 14-year-old son. The cause of death was officially cited as starvation, but the more obvious cause was a misunderstanding of the Bible.

Eric Cottam was 5-feet-10, yet he weighed only 69 pounds at the time of his death. He had not eaten any food for the last three weeks of his life because his parents refused to accept charity. They forbade Eric and his 12-year-old sister Laura to eat free meals at school. They refused to apply for welfare checks or food stamps or loans or charitable grants. They insisted that God would miraculously meet their needs as He saw fit. It took Eric's death to bring them to their senses, but by then it was too late.

"I don't hold God responsible," Larry Cottam told reporters. "The error was on my part, not God's."

How true. How sad. How tragic.

Younger sister Laura Cottam did not die, but she was diagnosed by hospital physicians to be suffering seriously from vitamin deficiencies, dehydration, and general malnutrition. Mr. and Mrs. Cottam told investigating police officers that they had eaten no food from November 22, 1988, to January 5, 1989. They were treated at Mercy Hospital in Wilkes-Barre before being taken to jail.

The ultimate irony of this true story is that besides being a truck driver, Larry Cottam was also an ordained minister. Furthermore, at the time his son starved to death, the Cottams owned two $50 U.S. Savings Bonds, they had $2131 in cash, their checking account had a $263 balance, and a local bank was holding $1281 of their money in an interest-earning passbook savings account! The Cottams told Pennsylvania State Trooper James J. Henry, Jr., that they couldn't use any of that money because it had been set aside as tithes and offerings for God, and as such it did not belong to them.

It is a bizarre twisting of logic for Christians to say on one hand that God owns the cattle on a thousand hills and that as a child of God those riches are the inheritance of all believers, and then on the other hand to say that a tithe to God cannot be used to save the life of a dying child! That is worse than inaccurate, it's criminal.

Correale F. Stevens, the District Attorney in Wilkes-Barre, said that the religious interpretations of Mr. and Mrs. Cottam were not adequate defenses for what they did to their boy. Said Stevens, "A son has died and he has died as the result of his parents' failure to provide him with the necessary life in terms of food, sustenance, and support."

In Luke 12:33, when Christ told His followers to "give alms," He was implying that a donation to the poor was a noble way to use one's money. What would be the point, however, of giving money to the needy if such people (like the Cottams) felt it was a sin to accept it? For a fact, it is not a sin to accept a helping hand. The sin is committed only when one abuses such kindness. God provides opportunities in a variety of ways, including help from friends and charities.

A story is often told about a man who was caught in a flash flood. He climbed on the roof of his house as the water continued to rise. He prayed, "Lord, deliver me from this calamity!"

In time, a crew of rescue workers arrived in a launch and threw him a rope. The man threw it back and said, "The Lord will deliver me."

Five minutes later his neighbor came by in a rowboat and tossed him a rope. The man rejected it and repeated, "The Lord will deliver me."

Fifteen minutes went by, and a helicopter came and dropped him a ladder. The man pushed it away and shouted, "The Lord will deliver me."

Just then the walls of the house collapsed and everything was washed away in the floodwaters. The man sank and drowned. When he arrived in heaven he confronted the Lord. "I prayed fervently to You. Why didn't You rescue me?"

"I sent two boats and a helicopter," the Lord answered. "What more did you want?"

What more indeed? Has it ever occurred to you that you might be playing out a version of that story right now in your own life? Only the punchline needs to be changed. When you ask the Lord why He never gave you a nice home or a new car or a vacation to Hawaii or a college education for your children, He might respond, "I gave you good health, citizenship in a free country, access to thousands of books in your local library, fellowship in a biblically sound church—what more did you want?" What more indeed?

Each Christian must assume a large element of responsibility for his or her own prosperity in life. God did not say to Adam, "Stand aside while I subdue the earth for you." He directed Adam to subdue it on his own, under the sanctions of God. That mandate is still in effect. The greater the effort, the greater the reward. The upside potential is left to each individual.

Money Itself Isn't Evil

I smile whenever a discussion begins about the risks that people run of turning evil after great wealth comes their way. Rich people are not out at nights burglarizing people's homes trying to obtain things they don't have but desperately want. Rich people are not out robbing liquor stores or mugging elderly ladies in alleys or stealing people's Social Security checks from their mailboxes.

Does this mean being rich makes one a good person? Does it mean being poor makes someone a bad person? The answer to both questions is no. Money does not create morals, but it does remove some basic temptations and fill most basic needs.

It is important to remember that the Bible states that the *love* of money (not money itself) is a root of every kind of evil (1 Timothy 6:10). The warning here is that a person who devotes his or her life to hoarding and amassing money just for the sake of accumulation is wasting the precious moments of life, not to mention passing up opportunities to provide blessings for others.

Still, money in a proper balance is a reassuring element in life. Remember the advice that Mr. Macawber gave young David Copperfield in the popular Dickens novel: "Annual income twenty pounds, annual expenditure nineteen pounds six, result happiness. Annual income twenty pounds, annual expenditure twenty pounds ought and six, result misery."

The lesson that mankind has learned over and over is that happiness cannot be purchased on credit, nor can it be bought with nonexistent money. Earning substantial funds leads to the enjoyment of substantial benefits. Good people will find good uses for their money, whatever it amounts to. Anyone who tries to argue against this fact will be hard-pressed to come up with solid evidence.

One Bible verse frequently cited is Mark 10:25, which says, "It is easier for a camel to go through the eye of a needle than for a rich man to enter the kingdom of God." What this verse was referring to was a narrow city gate which was nicknamed "Needle's Eye" because of the difficulty of bringing donkeys and camels through it when they had large baskets tied to their sides.

YOU CANNOT STAND STILL

Look at the problem of inflation and how it secretly robs you. In 1952 and 1953 the inflation rate for 24 months was only 1.5 percent. As such, what cost you $10 to buy in 1951 climbed to $10.15 by the end of 1953. In 1979 and 1980, however, the inflation rate for 24 months was 25.7 percent. So, what cost you $10 in 1978 had skyrocketed to $12.57 by the end of 1980. Wow! This means that if you received a 5 percent raise in both 1979 and 1980, you actually *lost* more than 15 percent of your money's buying power. Without understanding these factors, you might actually have thought that you were enjoying 10 percent more earning power.

Inflation is a zany rollercoaster. In 1972 it reached 12.2 percent, but by 1986 it was only 3 percent. A low inflation rate is not good news, though; it's just bad news to a lesser degree. If inflation stays at a moderate 6 percent per year, every 12 years you will lose half of the purchasing power of whatever your money is now worth. This means that if you put a thousand dollars in a passbook savings account that earned you 5½ percent interest per year, you would actually be *losing* buying power every year that you thought you were earning a profit. Now you know why we call times of tight money a depression. Thinking about it can depress anyone!

The point in all these references can be easily summarized. A God-honoring person will be God-honoring no matter what his station in life is, whether rich or poor. Nevertheless, extremes at either end will generate greater temptations. As such, it is dangerous to become obsessed with hoarding wealth for no purpose and it is equally dangerous to be so poverty-stricken that you feel driven to cheat or steal just to survive. We need balance—a balance secured by keeping the priorities and perspectives taught by Christ.

Everyone needs money, and it's time some Christian said it out loud. I don't mind being first: *Christians need money just like everyone else!* There is nothing holy about poverty, and there is nothing evil about wealth.

If we can learn to accept this fact, then the next move is to start right now in initiating a plan of action toward accumulating more money. If you feel hesitant about this or you don't feel the "time is right yet" for you to make your move, read on. I think I can change your mind.

I've often thought that there ought to be a separate little kingdom where all the procrastinators of the world could live. A perfect name for this place would be One Day Isle. The name would be borrowed from the conversation of the island's residents, whose most frequent expressions would be, "One day I'll...."

How about you? Would you qualify for citizenship on One Day Isle? Are you the sort of person who says, "One day I'll clean out this closet" or "One day I'll enroll in night school" or "One day I'll organize a home Bible study group"? If so, you probably also know that "one day" never seems to roll around. Procrastination moves responsibilities from "one day" to the next day, then to the next, and so on.

Ironically, what procrastinators don't seem to realize is that delaying a job will not make it easier to perform or cause it to go away. If anything, procrastination will compound the negative aspects of a task by adding time constraints and increasing tensions.

Pharaoh suffered through ten plagues before he finally took action to release the children of Israel. Jonah tried to delay his trip to Nineveh, and God punished him for his slack and cowardly ways. John Mark did not attend promptly to his duties, so Paul refused to let him travel with him anymore. The Bible has no praise for procrastinators. Instead it warns, "He who is slothful in his work is a brother to him who is a great destroyer" (Proverbs 18:9).

In 1928 twin brothers, age 25, received an inheritance of $2000 each. One brother announced that he was going to use his money to buy a plot of ground to develop into a farm. The other brother warned him to wait awhile, for rumors were afoot that a stock market crash was imminent. Better to sit tight and do nothing for a few years. Better to keep the money safe in a mattress.

But each brother followed his own plan and, sure enough, a year later the stock market crashed and the national economy went sour. The brother with the farm had to labor hard to plow and plant and weed his new land. The cautious brother still had his money in his mattress, however.

Some years later the first brother's farm was developed to full capacity and was earning great profits. The owner decided to invest his profits in a clothing factory. The second brother warned him, "Don't do it. There's a recession on its way. Sit tight. Wait awhile like I'm doing." But each brother followed his own advice and, sure enough, in 1938 a recession hit. The clothing factory had to cut its prices and work three shifts just to break even. The cautious brother still had his money in his mattress, however, and he lost nothing.

By 1941 the clothing factory had received several large orders to make military uniforms for soldiers during World War II. The factory's profits soared. The first brother decided to invest these extra profits in aircraft factories. The second brother warned him, "Don't do it. Before long the war will end and there will be no market for bombers and fighters. Sit tight. Wait it out like I'm doing." But each brother followed his own advice and, sure enough, in 1945 the war ended and all contracts for military aircraft were canceled. The aircraft factories had to devote many hours to converting their production lines to civilian passenger airplanes. This tied up the first brother's money, but the second brother's money was right at hand in the mattress where it always stayed.

By 1968 the aircraft factories were building satellites, rockets, and supersonic transports. Their profits were immense.

That year the two brothers retired. The cautious brother had his original $2000 . . . but nothing else. He had been correct in each of his predictions of pending disaster over the years, but what had it gained him? Nothing. Meanwhile, his hardworking brother had accumulated a prosperous farm, a garment business, and a string of airline factories. Even though his timing had always been bad, he had wound up a multimillionaire.

What made the difference here? The Bible explains it this way: "In all labor there is profit" (Proverbs 14:23). The slothful brother sought excuses to justify his inaction and procrastination. The diligent brother realized that there would never be a "perfect time" to start working, so he just jumped in right away. His work was blessed by God and rewarded accordingly.

Which brother do you resemble? Are you living on One Day Isle with the cautious brother, or are you building a boat to sail away with the diligent brother?

Each chapter in this book may be causing you to rethink many of the beliefs you have held for years. Hopefully you'll gain new and more positive insights on matters related to money management. Ultimately, whether or not you follow the advice given here will be your choice; and I respect your right to choose whatever course in life you feel is best for you. However, if you decide that what you are learning is right for you, I would encourage you to start right now to put these lessons into practice. As we emphasized in this chapter, there is nothing sinful about becoming prosperous, and there's no better time than right now to get started on the road to prosperity.

Chapter 6

Perspiration Versus Passivity: The Easy Way to Get Rich

There are two legal ways you can improve your financial status: You can *actively* earn more money by putting in overtime at your job or possibly even taking on a second job, or you can *passively* earn more money by having your money do your earning for you. The former procedure is known as *perspiration equity*; the latter is called *passive income*. The older you get, the more appealing passive income becomes to you, so the time to start generating it is *now*.

The joys of passive income become evident a lot sooner than you might imagine. I proved this with my son when he began to earn extra spending money at age 13 by mowing lawns. Where we live in Indiana the yards are big, so payment averaged about $20 per yard. I convinced my son to pay 10 percent of his earnings to our home church as a tithe and to invest an additional $5 out of every $20 in a mutual fund that was paying a 10 percent annual dividend.

I'll admit, the first summer my son invested this way was not a joyful time for him. He would slave away day after day at cutting, raking, and bagging grass, only to have me take $5 from him every time he got paid. These $5 payments eventually amounted to a $150 investment in his mutual fund by the end of that first summer (money he would rather have spent on records, a new basketball, comics, and a radio). The next summer we repeated the process (with equal amounts of griping). By the summer of his fifteenth birthday, however, his mutual fund had increased in value to $400 thanks to compounding interest.

One day, after receiving his monthly earnings statement, my son came into my office all excited. "Hey, Dad, check this out!" he said. "My mutual fund will be earning $40 in interest this year. That's like sitting at home watching television for two days and still earning the same amount of money I would have earned if I'd worked both days cutting lawns at $20 each!"

"Not bad, eh?" I said with a smile. "That's passive income, son. It only gets better. As the dividends compound upon themselves, the monthly earnings keep increasing. Soon, instead of two days off, it'll be equal to a week of lawn-mowing, then a month, and eventually the whole summer. The secret is to get started on it as soon as possible in life."

The same rule applies to you. Although the illustration of the lesson my son learned is minor in regard to the amount of money invested, the practice is valid on any level. What you sow, that shall you also reap. Invest a lot and you'll earn a lot. Invest a little and you'll earn a little. Invest nothing and you'll earn nothing.

If you are like my son and feel that earning money while watching television is more enjoyable than earning money while pushing a lawnmower in 90-degree heat all day, stay with me as we focus on ways that passive income can be generated.

The Specter of Debt

One of the first lessons you need to learn about passive income is that you can establish it for yourself (something positive) or you can provide it for other people (something negative). When you loan money to a bank by buying a certificate of deposit, your money earns interest and that is passive income for you. When you *borrow* money from a bank, you *pay* interest and that is passive income for the bankers. It is always more enjoyable to receive passive income than it is to pay interest! The key to the process is being able to get out of debt so that you can be a lender rather than a borrower.

Many Christians wrestle with the question of whether they should ever be in debt. Romans 13:8 says to "owe no one anything." Proverbs 17:18 implies that a person is devoid of understanding if he or she gets deeply in debt. Proverbs 22:7 says that a debtor is made to be in subjection to the lender.

When I am asked whether a Christian should ever be in debt, I respond with this answer: I feel it's perfectly all right for a Christian to owe a great deal of money as long as he remains cash-solvent. This means that even though a person may owe money for a home or car or furniture, he or she should also own enough property and other goods and investments to be able to pay off all his debts should a crisis ever arise. (Please note that even though bankruptcy is legal, it is not God-honoring, in my opinion.)

As an investor in stocks, I frequently buy stocks on margin. This means that I order and pay for stocks with my broker's money, which he loans to me at a fair-market rate of interest. As such, my personal stock portfolio may contain $60,000 worth of stocks, but $20,000 of that amount may be borrowed funds from my broker. Theoretically I'm in debt, but realistically I'm not. Why not? Because if my broker demanded the return of his loaned money, I could sell the stocks and give $20,000 to the broker (debt repaid) and keep $40,000 for myself. I am cash-solvent at all times because I own more money than I have borrowed.

Uncontrolled debt can be a dangerous thing: It can cause Christians to forgo tithing; it can create family tensions and cause marital disharmony; it can create carryover problems for children who inherit the debts of their parents.

People today have become oriented to the mindset "I want it, and I want it *now!*" Thanks to credit cards, it seems as though this sort of lifestyle might be very plausible. However, eventually those credit-card debts come due, and they have to be paid with real dollars. That's when, as one TV commentator has noted, "That drastic plastic isn't so elastic."

Most credit-card interest rates seem modest. You're told that the rate is only 2 percent per carryover month. After one year of that, however, you will be paying 24 percent annual interest *compounded monthly* at 2 percent of the total debt. Some finance companies charge as much as 36 percent compounded quarterly interest for auto loans and short-term debt. This means that if you were to borrow $4000 for two years you would pay back twice that amount. That is passive income running wild...and all against you. That's why it is important to control or eliminate debt.

Some people get so overwhelmed by debt that they don't know what to do about it. As a result, they take what little money they have and spend it on frivolous things in order to keep up appearances or to convince themselves things really aren't so bad. This is both naive and dangerous. If you really want to get out of debt, here's how.

1. Make a list of all your current debts and the percentage of interest you are paying on those debts. (See Figure 5, page 68.)

2. Send a letter to all your creditors and tell them you are in financial difficulty, but your intention is to repay

all your debts. Explain the token amount you can pay on each debt each month and enclose a check for the first payment.

3. After the token payments are paid for each creditor, take the bulk of your remaining money and pay it against your smallest bill. Do this each payday until that smallest bill is paid off. Follow the same procedure with the next-smallest bill, and on up the line until all your debts are paid.

4. Add no new debts to your existing list of debt items.

5. Keep a financial diary in which you write down every purchase you make. You'll be surprised to discover how many things you were buying that you really didn't want or need.

6. Live within a budget, but not one that is so restricted you can't enjoy a little fun now and then.

7. Pray and decide where your money should be spent wisely. Seek God's encouragement, strength, and guidance (Philippians 4:12,13).

8. Don't always buy things that are brand-new. Look for good used appliances in the want ads, buy toys at garage sales, take part in a church clothing exchange.

Always keep in mind that your goal is to get out of debt so that instead of using your money to make other people rich through passive income you can use it to make yourself rich through passive income. Be imaginative in your thinking about how to reduce debt. Control your money and discover ways to manage it more effectively.

Juggle your loans to reduce interest payments. If you have a personal loan of $10,000 on which you are paying 12 percent interest, you would be wise to borrow money from the cash value of your life insurance policies at a low rate of 3 to 8 percent and apply this money to the larger debt. If you borrowed $5000 at 5 percent from an insurance policy and paid it against your personal loan, you would then owe $5000 at 12 percent and $5000 at 5 percent. That would save you 7 percent of interest on that second $5000. At compounded quarterly interest rates, that means you would save about $360 in interest payments per year.

Continue to think about ways to generate money that can be applied to your debt. Every dollar applied to the principal owed on an outstanding loan will reduce both the debt load and the amount of future interest you will have to pay on that loan. That sort of progress will be very encouraging to you.

Learning to Save

As I mentioned before, it was difficult at first for my son to get into the habit of putting a portion of his lawn-mowing earnings into his mutual fund. If I had not been there to encourage him (*strongly* encourage, I might add) to save and invest, he might have skipped several payments. Today, however, he always makes a payment because he can see an immediate return value to himself.

You are no different from my son. Starting to save money and invest it for passive income benefits won't be easy at first. Here are some tips on how to encourage yourself to do it anyway.

1. If your employer will provide the service, have him automatically deposit part of your check into a payroll savings plan or a U.S. Savings Bond purchase program

(EE bonds are always exempt from city, county, and state taxes and they can sometimes also be exempt from federal taxes if used for college tuition) or a money market fund. You can't spend money you never get your hands on.

2. Pay cash whenever possible for purchases. If you do use a credit card, pay off the full balance when it comes due each month. For a copy of a list known as "Fair Deal Banks" (those that charge less than 17 percent interest on credit cards), send $1.50 to BankCard Holders of America, Suite 120, 560 Herndon Parkway, Herndon, Virginia 22070. The money you used to pay in interest can now be saved.

3. Reinvest your interest and dividends automatically rather than spend your earnings. This will increase the compounding effects of your earnings.

4. When you receive a Christmas bonus or an unexpected inheritance or a tax refund, put up to half of it in your savings rather than squandering it frivolously.

Whenever you begin any sort of savings and investing program, decide what sort of earnings rate you want to receive, as well as how much risk you can tolerate. If you want diversification because it scares you to have all your eggs in one basket, yet you don't have a great deal of money to invest, your best option is to invest in a couple of mutual funds. The funds will be invested in a variety of stocks and bonds so that there will be both stability and diversification. If you are a long-range investor and are very conservative, you may want to invest in Treasury bills, savings bonds, or certificates of deposit.

If, however, you want to be more aggressive in trying to accumulate passive income, you will need to be willing to invest in less secure but higher-yielding investments. We'll look at some of those later in this chapter, but first let's look at the person from whom you will be purchasing these investments.

Judging Your Broker

Many banks now run full-service brokerages that offer discount commissions similar to large discount brokerage firms, such as Charles Schwab & Company. Working with discount brokers saves you a great deal on commission costs and service fees, but it also puts the total responsibility on you for choosing which investments to purchase. For example, if you phoned your discount broker and asked, "What are five good growth stocks I should consider investing in?" the broker would respond, "I'm sorry, but we never make recommendations; we only fill orders."

A full-service broker, on the other hand, will spend time with you at his or her office or on the telephone giving you investment advice and answering your questions about stocks, bonds, and mutual funds. This broker will send you newsletters, brochures, and prospectuses to help you keep abreast of market shifts and investment opportunities. The commissions you pay will be from 25 to 40 percent higher, but some people feel it is well worth it because of the time they save by having someone else do all their research and work for them.

If you have ever read such novels as Theodore Dreiser's *The Financier* or Kenneth Lipper's *Wall Street* or Paul Erdman's *The Panic of '89*, you know that not all brokers and investment counselors have their clients' best interests at heart. A full-service broker has to sell more than $3,000,000 worth of investments each year in order to earn an annual salary of $48,000. To do this, some brokers resort to pressure talks, scare tactics, or a portfolio manipulation procedure called "churning." (Churning is the procedure of selling the profitable investments in your portfolio and then using the money to buy new investments. The broker earns a commission on the sale of the old investments *and* a commission on the purchase of the new investments. You, meanwhile, lose money both ways.)

Here are some tips on selecting a full-service broker. 1) Choose someone who has several years' experience in the business, is well-educated (CFP, CPA, MBA, or CLU), and has been with the same brokerage firm for at least three years. 2) Choose someone who is a good listener and will respond to your specific investment goals. 3) Choose someone who will talk openly about commission costs. 4) Choose someone who is able to adjust to your style of investing rather than someone who tries to push you into gambling on options or the futures market.

When I first began to invest in stocks, bonds, and mutual funds, I used a full-service broker. I learned a lot from this valuable experience. Today, however, I use a discount broker because I understand how the stock market works and I enjoy making my own investment decisions. Whichever way you decide to go, just remember that the ultimate responsibility of protecting your portfolio is your own. Passing the buck may mean losing it.

If you haven't developed an investing style yet that you are comfortable with, let me suggest that you give some thought to becoming a contrarian.

Contrarian Strategy

Have you ever tried the trick where you and a friend start to look up at the sky and a small crowd gathers around you and soon everyone else starts to look up too?

In psychology, this is known as the herd instinct—people want to do whatever everyone else is doing.

In nature most creatures like to stay in herds, flocks, gaggles, prides, or swarms. The few independent animals who disdain the safety of the group are called mavericks, rogues, or lone wolves. In investment circles, people who invest their money in the opposite direction of the majority of investors are called contrarians. When they win, they win in a big way; when they lose, they often lose everything. Being a contrarian is the fastest known way to become rich; it is also one of the fastest ways to go bankrupt. One must understand how the game is played.

Here's how contrarianism works: Suppose that the XYZ Chemical Company makes an announcement that instead of paying dividends for the next five years, it is going to sink all of its earnings into research on how to cure cancer (or grow hair or develop an AIDS vaccine). Most income-seeking investors would be upset at this news. They would sell their stock in XYZ Chemical, since it would no longer be paying dividends. If the stock had been selling at $15 per share, it might crash to $3 per share.

Contrarians, however, would feel that $3 per share is so cheap that it is worth risking some money on. Years later, if XYZ Chemical makes its breakthrough discovery, its stock would soar from $3 per share to $75 per share. The contrarians would make a fortune. Of course, if the chemical company fails to make a breakthrough, the contrarian would lose his investment. At only $3 per share, it would not be a tragic loss even at that, however. Contrarians feel it is well worth the risk.

In recent decades there have been some amazing opportunities for contrarians to invest their money. Let me use real examples to show you how it works.

During the 1970's, when the Chrysler Corporation

filed for reorganization, its stock became almost worthless. However, knowing that Lee Iacocca had been named the new president of Chrysler, some contrarians bought a lot of Chrysler stock at the cheap price of $4 per share. Three years later the stock had risen to $29 per share and the contrarians sold their stock for huge profits. (A purchase of 5000 shares at $4 would have cost $20,000. Selling the 5000 shares at $29 would have returned $145,000. That's a 625 percent return on investment!)

Conversely, during the early 1980's when Braniff Airlines lost much of its public credibility, causing its shares to sink to record lows, the contrarians bought up huge blocks of this inexpensive stock. Instead of "flying high" again, however, the stock crashed. Braniff declared bankruptcy and its stock became worthless. The contrarians lost everything.

Although contrarian investing is risky, its procedures are worth understanding. My personal contrarian investing follows a set pattern: If a solid and stable corporation experiences a decline in value in its stock due to overall market conditions, I buy substantial amounts of that stock and then hold it for as long as it takes for the stock to regain its value.

In September 1987 a share of Commonwealth-Edison Power & Electric Company (a major utility) was selling for $37 per share. When the famous October 10, 1987, crash occurred on Wall Street, the value of Commonwealth-Edison nosedived to $24 per share. This was a ridiculously low price for this stock, since the stock was paying a $3-per-share dividend. Also, Commonwealth was selling a product (power) that people had to have. I didn't need to be much of a financial analyst to realize that once the panic selling of *all* stocks ceased and people started to get back into the market, they would turn first to dependable stocks like "Comm-Ed." This would drive the price back up.

So, when everyone else was selling, I started buying. I bought 1000 shares of Comm-Ed at $25.50 per share. By a year later I had earned $3000 in dividends *and* the stock had increased from $25.50 to $31 per share. I sold out at a $5.50 per share profit. That gave me $5500 in markup value plus $3000 in dividends for a total profit of $8500. I bought a new computer, paid in advance for both of my children's tuition at a private Christian school, and then took my wife on a vacation to Honolulu for a week. Like I said before, when a contrarian wins, that person wins in a big way.

My advice on contrarian investing is as follows: 1) Do not invest money you cannot afford to lose, such as your retirement funds; 2) purchase stocks of blue-chip companies whenever the market has driven prices down because of external emotional circumstances (such as when Operation Desert Shield was initiated in 1990); 3) try to select stocks that will pay you a dependable dividend no matter what price the stock is selling for; 4) whenever prices rise substantially, don't get greedy— sell out at a good profit; and 5) whenever prices start to fall substantially, don't start to panic but consider buying even more stock so that your upside potential will be even greater.

Keep in mind that a salmon that swims upstream has a rough go of it, but it eventually reaches cool, calm, refreshing waters. Going against the financial current can be equally rough, but the rewards are equally beneficial.

For those of you who want these higher returns, but just don't have the stomach for the risks that a contrarian must take, there are some other investments worth considering: hybrid certificates of deposit, convertible municipal zero bonds, and "junk" bonds. Each one of these is like a contrarian stock purchase in that it carries a risk, but each also carries a large reward for the investor who learns to purchase it wisely. Let's examine them individually.

Hybrid Certificates of Deposit

The first generation of certificates of deposit (CD's) was designed to provide safety and a guaranteed predictable return on investment. Generally, they worked like this: The investor would invest a specific amount of money (usually $500 minimum) for a specific time period (from 3 to 60 months). Whereas a passbook savings account might be paying only 5 percent, CD's could offer rates of 7 to 10 percent. Naturally, there was a penalty if the money was withdrawn prior to the agreed-upon maturity date. Since most credit unions and banks insured CD's with the federal government for up to $100,000 per account holder, the CD's were—and still are—very secure.

Since 1986 a second generation of CD's has been developed. Unlike the standard CD's that provide guaranteed predictable interest earnings, these new CD's are extremely unpredictable. They have the potential to make an investor very wealthy or very poor, depending on how the U.S. economy rises or falls. The reason for this is because the new CD's are linked in value to fluctuating factors, such as inflation or stock market prices or the prime rate of interest. Let's examine some of these second-generation CD's.

The "bump-up CD" is a no-penalty rollover certificate. What you do is buy a CD from a bank with the understanding that if the bank ever offers a higher interest rate for its future CD's, you will be allowed to cash in your first CD and use those funds to buy the higher-yielding CD. For example, let's suppose that in 1990 you bought a $1000 bump-up CD with a five-year maturity at a rate of 7 percent interest. If in 1992 the bank started to offer the CD's with five-year maturities at 8 percent interest, you could trade your 7 percent CD for a new 8 percent CD.

GLOSSARY OF INVESTMENT JARGON

Bonds. Bonds are paper contracts which guarantee to pay back a specific amount of cash to the lender at a fixed interest rate on a specified date in the future. Bonds are issued by city, state, or federal governments or by corporations. Their prices fluctuate according to economic trends or corporate needs for immediate cash flow (as in selling "junk bonds" at inflated rates to finance a leveraged buyout).

CD's. Certificates of Deposit are issued by savings and loans associations or by state or federal banks. They are guaranteed agreements by the institution to pay back an investor's principal plus a predetermined amount of interest earnings.

Commercial paper. Short-term promissory notes (often not secured by tangible assets) are termed commercial paper. They are loans made to corporations that earn set rates of interest.

DJIA. The Dow-Jones Industrial Average is a daily averaging of 30 stocks whose fluctuations somewhat reflect the overall movement of the total stock market.

Earnings. In the broadest sense, any appreciation in value of an investment vehicle is deemed earnings for the investor. Examples include interest on CD's, stock dividends, rise in real estate value, and bond coupon payments.

Prime rate. The interest rate charged by banks to their prime (most valued) customers for short-term loans is called the prime rate.

Principal. The base amount of cash that is put into an investment is known as the principal.

S & P 500. The Standard & Poor's 500 Price Index is a daily averaging of 50 utility stocks, 425 industrial stocks, and 25 transportation stocks to determine the broad-range fluctuations of stock market prices.

Stocks. All stock represents partial ownership of a company. *Preferred* stock pays a set rate of dividend and has a claim ahead of common stock on the company's assets in the event of dissolution. *Common* stock entitles the holder to receive dividends and to vote on company business. It has greater potential for upside appreciation in value.

The advantage of a bump-up is that you will never be locked in at low rates if interest starts to climb. There are three disadvantages, however: 1) You cannot bump up your CD from one bank to a different bank that is paying higher interest unless you cash out the first CD and pay a penalty charge; 2) each time you bump up to a new CD you will usually have to start from day one in working toward your ultimate maturity date; and 3) since bump-up rates can be costly to banks, the bump-up CD's pay a slightly lower initial rate of interest than standard CD's.

Another kind of CD is the "Gold Rate Certificate of Deposit." This is a CD with an interest yield related to the price of gold. If gold is at $400 an ounce, your CD might pay around 7 percent interest. If gold falls to $350 an ounce, your CD interest will drop to about 4 percent. If gold rises to $600 an ounce, your CD will pay about 11 percent interest.

The "S & P Rate CD" is a CD with an interest yield related to the Standard and Poor's 500-stock index. This was first offered in 1987 by Chase Manhattan Bank. Sometimes the stock market performed so well that investors earned a 7 percent rate of interest; at other times, however, the market was so depressed that investors earned no interest at all on these CD's.

The "Inflation-Plus CD" is a CD that pays the investor a 2 to 5 percent margin over current inflation rates. For example, if in 1990 you purchased an Inflation-Plus CD for $10,000 with a four-year maturity date at a guaranteed 3 percent return above inflation, you would earn 10 percent interest if inflation stayed at 7 percent. At first glance this sounds like a really safe investment, since you know that you'll always be ahead of each year's inflation rate. There are drawbacks, however.

The Inflation-Plus CD usually requires a $10,000 minimum investment, and if you draw it out prior to the full maturity date the bank can withhold up to six months' interest earnings as a penalty charge. Furthermore, if the national inflation rate drops to 2 percent, as it did during part of the Reagan administration, your $10,000 would only earn 5 percent interest. That's a worse rate than a passbook savings account. Of course, if inflation soared to 17 percent, as it did during the Carter administration, you could earn 20 percent interest on your CD.

A variety of other CD's are also available. The "College-Sure CD" has interest rates tied to the College Board Index of college costs. The "Real Estate CD" has rates tied to statewide and regional real estate values.

My personal belief is that every portfolio should have a certain amount of guaranteed assets in it, such as standard CD's. My strategy has been to buy several small ($250 to $500) conventional CD's with staggered maturity dates between one and five years. In this way I'm always close to a maturity date in case I have forthcoming financial needs, and I'm not extended too far into the future in case interest rates should start to rise.

Convertible Municipal Zeros

Municipal bonds provide tax-free earnings on the federal and often the state and city and county government levels. One way of extending these earnings is by purchasing convertible municipal zero coupon bonds. These bonds are sold at a discount to par value and they mature at full value after ten or more years. However, when the bond matures, it automatically converts to a conventional bond that pays coupon interest for yet another ten years. The purchaser ends up receiving federally *untaxed* earnings accumulations as the bond ages toward maturity, and then after maturity the purchaser receives federally untaxed income. When ordering convertible municipal zeros, look for an investment rating of A, AA, or AAA by an independent rating agency. Also, make sure that the bond can't be "called" for at least five years, so that the momentum of your interest earnings will have time to accumulate a substantial fund.

Junk Bonds

There's an adage in investing that says, "The greater the risk, the greater the return." This is particularly true in the high-yield corporate bond markets. Whenever the independent credit evaluating services, such as Moody's or Standard & Poor's, rate a bond in the A range, it means there is very little risk that this bond will lose its value (or that the corporation selling it will default on payment). Because of its solid security, it will pay an average of only 7 to 10 percent interest. These payments are usually calculated every six months and a payment check ("dividend") is then mailed to the owner of the bond.

If a bond carries a lower rating (such as BB for Standard & Poor's or Ba for Moody's), this means it is riskier to invest your money in this bond. Brokers use the nickname "junk bonds" for these bonds. To compensate for this risk, the corporation pays a higher rate of interest. For example, when National Medical Enterprises put bonds up for sale at $1000 per bond with a maturity date in the year 2000, the bonds were rated Baa1 by Moody's. Consequently the bonds offered a 12.1 percent rate of interest. If the investor was willing to invest $1000 in this marginally risky corporation, he or she would receive $121 interest each year. If the bond was purchased in 1989 and held for 11 years until its maturity date, the investor would receive the $1000 principal back, plus along the way would receive $1331 in dividends. Thus, through passive income, the investor would have more than doubled his or her money.

The reason corporations sell bonds is because they want to raise capital (ready cash) without having to sell off part of their company in doing so (more shares of stock). For example, Bethlehem Steel lost money from 1982-86. To maintain cash flow the company sold bonds that paid a 9 percent interest rate through their maturity year of 2000. When the company became very profitable again in 1987 and 1988, the ratings on the bonds were improved by Moody's.

Many bonds can be "called" before their maturity date. This means that if interest rates drop and the government agency or private corporation that issued your bond wants to redeem it, it can send your principal investment amount back to you. At that point your bond is fully refunded. Your interest stops coming in.

Bonds can be purchased through your stockbroker. The price you pay for a bond can be at, below, or above the $1000 face value, depending on current interest rates. For example, if a bond offers to pay 10 percent interest while other investments are paying only 9 percent, then you'll have to pay a little more than $1000 in order to buy such a top-earning investment. However, if the bond is paying 10 percent while other investments are paying 11 percent, you can buy it at a discount because it's not as profitable as other investments. The discount rate helps compensate you for the loss difference.

Junk bonds are not nearly as risky as many people believe. In 1984 not even 1 percent of all outstanding bonds experienced a default problem, and even those that did were able to return at least 40 percent of the amount that people had invested.

When determining which corporations to purchase high-yield bonds from, look for these key factors: Find a company that is working hard to reduce its existing debt; find a company that owns land, buildings, and other assets that can be sold to pay debt; find a company that uses its income to improve efficiency and increase its business.

The more eager you are to obtain wealth, the more risk tolerance you are going to need. Junk bonds offer excellent returns—just do your homework first.

And that can be a byword for this entire chapter. Homework, or careful checking, on investments helps you understand what you are doing and gives you confidence in making your decisions. From that point on it's all passive gains!

Chapter 7

Paying Hobbies and Other Fun Investments

During the year my son was a sophomore in high school, each student in the tenth grade was given a 20-dollar bill. All were told to use the money as they saw fit to increase it on behalf of their private Christian school, and then to return the original $20 and all earned profits to the school at the end of one year.

It was fascinating to see some of the ways the students invested the seed money in order to make it grow. Two brothers put their money together and bought rags, soap, and sponges and then held car washes on several weekends. They increased the $20 to $125.

One girl bought craft materials and made Christmas ornaments which she sold at a neighborhood bazaar. She increased her $20 to $85. Another girl spent her money to make fliers advertising her services as a babysitter. She made a $75 profit. Another girl bought flour, sugar, and other baking goods and made cookies which she sold for a good profit.

At the end of the year the students had learned two valuable lessons: First, that even a little bit of money can become profitable if it is used cleverly, and second, that making money can often be fun!

I too had learned this lesson as a youngster. My father was a very busy man and often had to work late at his office. On Friday nights, however, he made it a practice to come home at 6 P.M. sharp. With him would be a large sack of pennies. He would stop by the bank to cash his paycheck and, while there, would also have them give him 20 rolls of pennies. After dinner on Friday nights, my brother Gary, my dad, and I would sit on the living room floor, unwrap the pennies, dump them into a big pile, and then start to examine them one by one.

My father would pick up a penny and announce what its date and mint mark were, and then my brother and I would run a check on it. First my brother would see if it was a penny we needed in order to fill a slot in one of the coin folders we had purchased at the coin shop. If it was one we needed, he would tell my dad and my dad would pass it to Gary to insert into the album. If it was a coin we already had, my dad would announce a judgment as to its condition (such as uncirculated, very good, or poor) and if it was better than the coin we already had in the album, we would swap coins and upgrade the quality of our collection. I would then use the coin book to see if the coin we were replacing was worth saving, trading, selling, or just returning to the bank.

We spent hours upon hours doing this. We had the time of our lives just being together as "the men of the family," and it was also like being on a treasure hunt. Every so often we would make a real find, such as the time we came up with a 1931-S (San Francisco mint) penny which we sold the next day for $25 at the coin shop.

We kept our collections for years, eventually expanding into nickels, dimes, quarters, Indian head pennies, and proof coins. Along the way we learned a lot about American government and history, we had a good time of family fellowship as we built our collections together, and we accumulated an overall collection that later amounted to several hundred dollars in value. Even though it was my dad who did most of the bankrolling for this venture (he bought the rolls of pennies each week), he always insisted that the collection belonged to "the boys." Years later we were able to liquidate the coin collection to pay for some of our college expenses.

The Fun Part of Making Money

My point in relating these stories is to show you that making money can be something you enjoy doing if you link it to a hobby, project, or favorite pastime. If you can't imagine yourself as someone who studies *The Wall Street Journal* each morning in an effort to spot a good stock or bond offering, you might be just as successful if you invested your money in a collection of rare porcelain dolls or Civil War artifacts or into the makings of a small business related to sewing, crafts, models, sports, or amusements.

Let me share a few stories with you about people I know who have had fun making money because they tied it to something they enjoyed doing.

Hal Souers of Warren, Indiana, is one of 3000 Americans who invest in Hudson automobiles for both long- and short-range profits. What makes Hal stand out among the 3000 people is that he began buying Hudsons even before he was old enough to drive one. He purchased a "junk heap" Hudson for $54 at an auction when he was 15 years old. Nine years later, at age 24, Hal Souers owned 84 Hudsons which he kept in rows in a field behind the big farmhouse he grew up in. It has proven to be a very profitable hobby and business for Hal. In 1986 he spent $1200 buying junk heap Hudsons, stripping them for parts, and then using the parts to restore a 1954 Hudson Hornet which he sold for $10,000. By day Hal works as a farmer, but at night and on weekends he tinkers. To date his tinkering has netted him somewhere in the neighborhood of $90,000.

"My grandpa had a 1939 Hudson Terraplane that he bought new and kept for decades," says Hal. "I used to

love to ride with him in that big old car. I'd go to the
library and get books about the history of automobile-
making and I'd read all I could about the Hudson Company (1909-1956)."

Hal studied auto mechanics in high school machine
shop class and learned more about engines from his
father and brothers. During the summers he would go to
car auctions, buy old Hudsons, have his dad haul them
home for him, and then start restoring them as best he
could. Through a national periodical called *Hudson
Auto Collector's Newsletter*, Hal learned how to find car
parts at reasonable prices and how to sell his restored
cars once he was finished with them.

"People kept telling me how impressive it was that I
was making such large profits," recalls Hal, "but what
they didn't realize was that I was having a great time
rebuilding those cars. It was a lot of fun, and I happened
to be able to generate a lot of cash at the same time."

At one point in 1988 Hal Souers had five Hudsons that
he had restored at mint condition. Each had a market
value of from $11,000 to $20,000. Hal called these five
cars his "personal collection," which he defined as mean-
ing "cars that I love to own and drive and display at car
shows for trophies and cash prizes . . . cars that will stay
in my personal collection until someone is willing to pay
the premium price I've set on them."

That Junk in Your Attic May Be Valuable

Several people have told me stories about how their
hobbies accidentally became investment vehicles. A
deacon at my church named Jim Clark used to collect
baseball cards as a kid, as most boys do. However, Jim
never threw his cards away when he got older. He put
them in albums and stored them in a back closet. After
he got married and started raising his family and had a
son of his own, he became interested in baseball cards

again. To his amazement, an entire culture of baseball card fanatics had developed in recent years. His old cards now had great value to contemporary collectors. Jim resisted the temptation to sell out and grab the quick money. Instead, he kept the cards he had and began to buy and save new cards with his son. Today they have a huge collection that they save, trade, sell, and barter with at trade shows. Each year the value goes up, but each year Jim and Jonathan continue to have fun wheeling and dealing with their collection.

One of the Sunday school teachers at my church grew up in Kentucky, where whittling and knife-swapping were common pastimes. From this heritage, Jim Middleton developed an interest in specialty pocket knives. He began to buy one knife per month through specialty catalogs or at gun and knife shows. Some of his knives he put on display, some he used, and some he kept for bargaining and trading with other collectors. To Jim it was enjoyable knowing the history of how a certain kind of knife was designed, used, refined, and marketed. By buying at a steady but not budget-breaking rate, Jim has accumulated a knife collection which today is diversified, useful and very valuable.

One woman at my church, Mary Kimpel, and her late husband, Gene, began a hobby of collecting antiques in 1975 which eventually led to the finding of some valuable items. Gene used to tell me that the secret to successful antique-collecting was to keep in mind that one person's junk was another person's lost treasure.

Gene had started a collection of antique light fixtures which he repaired in his basement work area. He put some of them into use around his own house. He did not want to invest a lot of money in his collection, so he learned how to swap, dicker, and bargain-hunt. For example, he once discovered a bunch of Depression Era metal toys in the attic of one of his relatives. He asked if the relative wanted them and was told, no, he could have them. Gene then looked in *Antique Journal* magazine for someone who was seeking Depression Era toys. He contacted that person and asked if she had any antique light fixtures. She said yes, and she and Gene swapped items. No money was exchanged, yet her toy collection immediately rose in value and Gene's light-fixture collection also rose in value. It was a win-win situation.

"In the 12 years before Gene's death, we had a lot of fun doing our antique-collecting," says Mary Kimpel. "We would walk around flea markets and antique shows or take a day to visit rummage sales or farm liquidations. We would haggle over prices and ask information about old items and just have fun seeing so many historical things. It was cheap entertainment, and we came out very well financially. I always tell people to look for a gold mine up in their attics. It might be disguised as a hope chest from sister Jane or a photo album from Aunt Sue or some flapper clothes and jewelry once worn by Granny."

Knowing Book Value

In 1970 a friend of mine named Dick Weiderman decided that he would like to have a personal collection of all of the 58 books written by American author Jack London (1876-1916). Dick was a great fan of London's writings, and as a high school English teacher he also read and taught London's stories and novels to his students.

Dick ran an inexpensive classified ad in the city newspaper where he resided in Grand Rapids, Michigan. He said he was interested in buying hardback copies of Jack London books. More than 40 people called to say that they had books they would like to get rid of.

"I was really surprised by the response," recalls Dick. "Folks had old books by Jack London stored in attics, basements, garage lofts, home libraries, offices, hunting lodges, and summer cabins. Some people just gave them to me. Others looked at the original price of the book (usually $1.50 to $2.00) and charged me that. A few asked me for big payments, and I just said no and left."

Dick wound up with about 350 editions of various Jack London books. His total cost was under $100. Some of the books were damaged beyond current use, so he had to discard them. Others were cheap reprints which he kept as "trading" copies when dealing with owners of used bookstores. Others, however, were first-edition books in excellent condition.

"I immediately fell in love with the first-edition books," admits Dick. "The book paper was thick, the print was large, the page borders were wide, and the illustrations were gorgeous. I made up my mind that I didn't just want a copy of each of London's books, but I wanted an actual first-edition, excellent-condition copy of each of his books. It became a hobby for me to secure these first editions."

Dick went to the library and checked out a book called *Guide to Small Presses* and discovered there were three small-circulation quarterly journals being published about the writings of Jack London. He subscribed to all three. He also found a book called *Jack London First Editions* by James E. Sisson III that helped him know how to recognize genuine first-edition copies of London's works and how to determine their current market value.

Dick was amazed to discover that some of the books he had purchased for just a few dollars were worth from $50 to $175 or more. He began to spend his weekends driving to neighboring towns to visit used bookstores in search of more first editions or trading copies.

"I learned from the London quarterly journals that there was a Jack London bookstore in Glen Ellen, California, that would take my extra copies in trade toward expensive editions I needed to purchase for my collection," explains Dick. "This sort of bartering helped me to get rare titles at below-market prices."

Dick spent five years completing (and reading) his collection. One of his London books, *The Cruise of the Dazzler*, is valued at $4500 because of its quality and scarcity. The total collection when completed had cost Dick about $3800, but its market value as a compiled set was approximately $17,250. Today it is worth even more, but it sits in Dick's private home library (under lock and key and protected by an alarm system), where its value increases each year. Dick considers it his "bonus retirement money" for when he decides to leave the field of teaching.

How It Is Done for Fun

In each one of these stories we discovered some common factors. First, the person doing the collecting chose an area that he or she could have some fun doing so that the "investing" would be a happy event and not a drudgery. As such, don't just start collecting stamps or campaign buttons or old movie posters because their value will increase over time; collect something that you can learn from, use, be entertained by, or share with someone else. This will motivate you to keep working with your investment.

Second, each person in our stories always tried to improve the level of quality of whatever was being collected. Hal Souers upgraded the serviceability of his Hudsons; Dick Weiderman replaced cheap reprint books with excellent first editions; my brother and I replaced well-worn pennies with shiny uncirculated ones. The collectors did this replacing by trading, bartering, doing legwork in tracking down items, and seeking cost-effective ways of upgrading a collection without expending great amounts of cash.

Third, these collectors did self-study about the items they were collecting. Dick Weiderman subscribed to journals about Jack London books, and Hal Souers read books and a newsletter about Hudson cars. Gene and Mary Kimpel read magazines about antiques and also asked people at antique sales to teach them how to evaluate historical artifacts. Jim and Jonathan Clark went to trade shows related to collecting baseball cards and talked with dealers and other collectors. It is important to keep current in the hobby area in which you plan to invest your time and money.

And fourth, these collectors were never in a hurry to sell their collections. Patience and timing are crucial in earning a maximum return on collectible items. Hal Souers chose to drive his Hudson cars until someone was willing to meet his price. Dick Weiderman is reading his London books and keeping them on display until he decides the time is right to sell them. Jim Middleton sells his knives when demand rises for one style over another.

If you want to ease into the world of investments rather than jump in all at once, one way to start is to spend more time enhancing a hobby or collection you're fond of. Think of it as being paid to have a good time!

Chapter 8

Estate Planning This Side of Heaven

In our final chapter we need to discuss estate planning. Now before you close the book and say, "I don't need to read this chapter because I haven't made enough to worry about," you need to realize that *everybody* has an estate. You may not have a large enough estate to be taxable, but you do have an estate nevertheless, and it needs your attention.

Your "estate" is the sum of all your assets after all debts have been paid (and all donations to charity have been made). Only estates worth more than $600,000 pay estate tax (at rates from 37 to 55 percent). A husband and wife can leave a total of $1,200,000 tax-free if they arrange it in such a way that each is seen to be leaving $600,000.

To analyze the capital (money value) of your estate you must project your future cash needs by comparing your current income to your retirement goals. The "Estate Capital Analysis" chart in this chapter (Figure 7, page 134) will show you how to do this. The "Objectives of Estate Planning" chart (Figure 8, page 135) will help you itemize the payments your estate will need to make upon your death in order to bury you, pay off the debts you leave behind, and award the bequests you have outlined in your will.

It used to be that the only people who gave thought to protecting their income and property through estate planning were those who lived on large "estates" with a mansion, beautiful furnishings, many acres of land, and big bank accounts. Today, however, estate planning is appropriate even for apartment-dwellers who live on a fixed income.

People in the United States are wealthier than 80 percent of the rest of the world's population. Americans accumulate furnishings, real estate, cars, fine jewelry, paintings, insurance policies, mink coats, and many other tangible assets. Upon retirement they want those goods to serve them, and at death they want those items to be passed on to their heirs or chosen beneficiaries. To guarantee this, an element of estate planning is necessary.

The first step is to have a will drawn up by your family attorney. This not only spells out your desires about the disbursement of your estate, but it also reduces the number of disagreements among surviving beneficiaries. It also prevents the state from stepping in and settling the estate for you. If you wish to establish trusts for loved ones or worthy institutions, you should designate how these trusts are to be funded, monitored, and administered.

The second step is to do a complete analysis of your tax situation. The "Income Tax Analysis" form (Figure 9, page 136) and the "Tax Summary Analysis" chart (Figure 10, page 137) will show you how to do this. Often you can greatly reduce your tax payments while simultaneously improving your estate planning objectives. This is because the two overlap; for example, payments made to your Individual Retirement Account are tax-deductible, but they also earn cash for your future retirement.

One question that often arises when tax shelters and estate planning are discussed is, "Can I reduce my tax burden by donating some of my money to Christian organizations?" The answer is a resounding *yes*! Here's one example of how I personally have done this.

Most people know that the money they contribute to churches and missionary groups and other charitable organizations is tax-deductible if the taxpayers use the IRS long form for itemized deduction listings. However, what is just as important to know is that the donor can also have some control over the use of the money without losing the deduction. I proved this through the purchase of life insurance on myself, funded by me but owned by my church.

I asked our pastor and deacon board to buy a $25,000 life insurance policy on me. The initial premium was $280, which I donated to the church; then the church in turn paid it to the life insurance company. Now I will continue to pay this same donation to the church for the next seven years so that the annual premiums can be made. After seven years there will be enough cash value built up in the account so that the interest earnings can pay for the premiums from there on out.

I will receive a $280 tax deduction each year that I donate the premium payment amount to my church ($280 x 7 = $1960). Whenever I die, the church will receive $25,000 to assist its continued ministry. So while raising $25,000 for my church I have gained a $1960 tax deduction for myself.

Your insurance agent or church treasurer can help you explore a variety of other ways in which you can channel your tax-deductible dollars into organizations that are doing God's work. Religiously oriented colleges often have estate planners who can also help you in this area.

Your third step is to review your Social Security status. Even though most wage-earners complain continually about having Social Security payments withdrawn from their paychecks, statistically speaking it is one of the best investments toward retirement that most people ever make. For example, research shows that if a woman retires at 65 and lives to be 80, she will draw out 1000 to 2000 percent more cash than she ever paid in! What other investment are you into right now that can guarantee to pay you up to 20 times your investment? None! Social Security is really not a bad deal at all.

To make sure that your Social Security records are correct, you should compare your name and Social Security number with the name and number on your pay stubs during December and on the W-2 form you receive in January. The name *and* number should be identical on all of these documents. The W-2 form is the primary means of crediting earnings to your Social Security earnings record. Each year earnings are credited to records by matching the name and number on the W-2. Earnings are sometimes not credited because an incorrect name or number throws off the computer system.

The Social Security Administration is a highly automated organization headquartered in Baltimore, Maryland. Despite its technical equipment, it can make errors. Because of this, the SSA suggests that you run a check on your personal account every three to five years.

Checking is easy. Just phone toll-free 1-800-937-2000 or obtain form SS-7004, "Request for Social Security Statement of Earnings," from any Social Security office. As you fill out the card, you can also write in "Please furnish a benefit estimate" if you want to be told what your monthly payment will probably be once you reach age 65.

Your statement will be sent to you in about one month. It will list your yearly total of credited earnings for the previous four years. All yearly totals prior to that will be lumped into one grand total. For self-employed people these totals can date back to 1951 and for wage-earners as far back as 1937. Earnings prior to 1937 do not count.

Should you discover a mistake in your records, assemble your documents of proof and immediately report all errors to your local Social Security office. The most convincing documents that can be used to substantiate your argument are copies of your previous tax returns and the W-2 forms that show how much you paid in FICA taxes in specific years. Keep the government on its toes by double-checking all figures and records. It's your money; guard it.

The fourth procedure is to get involved in a company pension plan or to start paying into an IRA (Individual Retirement Arrangement). If you are a wage-earner, your employer will be the one to help you review your pension options. If you are self-employed, an IRA is for you.

The 1986 Tax Reform Act made sweeping changes in the laws regulating IRA's. Of the 40 million Americans who were investing regularly in IRA's, nearly 15 million were no longer eligible and another 8 million were eligible for only a partial deduction. Here are the new guidelines for people who are *not* involved in a company-sponsored or organization retirement plan.

A. Unmarried individuals can make tax-deductible contributions to an IRA up to $2000 annually, no matter how high one's earning level is.

B. If an employed person is married and his or her spouse is also employed but neither is covered by a qualified retirement plan, both spouses can make up to $2000 in annual tax-deductible IRA contributions no matter how high their individual or joint earnings are.

C. If an employed married person has a spouse who is unemployed, the married worker can make annual tax deductible contributions up to $2000 to his or her personal IRA and up to $250 to a spousal IRA.

For persons *with* qualified retirement plans, here are the revised rules.

A. Unmarried individuals with qualified retirement plans can deduct $2000 annually for contributions to an IRA if they earn less than $25,000 annually. Between earnings of $25,000 and $35,000 the deductions are reduced according to one's adjusted gross income. Beyond $35,000 no deductions are allowed.

B. If either spouse in a marriage is covered by a qualified retirement plan and the couple files a joint return, no tax deductions may be taken for contributions to an IRA if the couple earns more than $50,000 of adjusted gross income. The full $4000 for a working couple or $2250 for a couple with one working spouse may be deducted if the combined earnings (AGI) are under $40,000. Income above $40,000 reduces the deduction by $200 for every $1000 of additional income.

Insights on Life Insurance

With as many life insurance options as there are available today it is not at all surprising that many people postpone any decision regarding which policy to purchase. Unfortunately, such a delay can sometimes find you *dead* wrong in your decision to procrastinate! But buying life insurance does not have to be a weighty problem. It can be reduced to a one-step action if you become informed about universal life (or "variable life") policies.

Let me begin by explaining that in a very real sense all life insurance is *term* insurance. Usually people think of insurance as being either "term" insurance or "whole-life" insurance.

Term insurance is a product in which the death benefit of the policy remains the same until death but the premiums increase each year (or decade) that you grow older, or else the reverse, in that the premiums never increase but the death benefit of the policy decreases each year until it is ultimately worthless and no longer in force. There is no cash value to term insurance policies because they hold no cash in the account. As such, you cannot borrow money out of these policies nor can you cash them in for a lump sum payment prior to death.

Whole-life insurance is a product that charges you a substantially higher premium for the same amount of death benefit coverage as you would receive in a term insurance policy. However, once established, these annual premiums never increase nor does the death-benefit coverage of the policy ever decrease. Additionally, as cash builds up inside the policy, the owner may borrow a portion of this money from the policy at a rate of interest below bank and savings and loan rates. The policy can also be "turned in" for a specified amount of cash value if the owner no longer wishes to keep the policy in force.

One way or the other, the purchaser of a life insurance policy is going to have to pay adequate payments so that the insurance company's risk factor is constant no matter which type of policy is purchased. Since all policies are eventually either canceled or redeemed after a certain term of years, all insurance policies wind up being term insurance. (Let's hope that your term of years on this earth is long; but if not, let's hope that you *do* have some form of insurance in force at the time of your death.)

Predictions of longevity (known as actuarial science) have been around for more than 300 years. One of the first students of this estimation process was Edmund Halley (1656-1742), the statistician who is credited with discovering and charting Halley's Comet. With accurate longevity tables in hand, most insurance companies prospered very well by playing the long odds on policyholders. However, around 1975 the odds took a radical shift in favor of the policyholders and caused some insurance companies to suffer severe financial setbacks. Some even went out of business.

Here is what happened: When double-digit interest rates were prevalent, people who owned whole-life policies saw this as a golden opportunity to leverage their cash. They borrowed all the money they were entitled to borrow out of their whole-life policies. Depending on the size of the policy and the number of years it had been in force, these loans ranged from a few hundred dollars to as high as tens of thousands of dollars. The wonderful aspect about these loans was that when the policy had been written (prior to the inflation panic of the late 1970's), the company agreed to loan the money in the policy back to the policyowner at the incredible low rates of 2 to 5 percent interest *and* the policy would stay in full force. If death occurred before the loan was paid off, the balance due would be deducted from the principal due at death and all remaining money would be sent to the policy's beneficiary.

Knowing this, people borrowed money from their insurance policy at around 3 percent interest and invested it at 16 percent quarterly compounded interest in ten-year certificates of deposit. Financial advisers and accountants were advising people to do this. The cash-flow drain on the insurance companies was devastating. Even worse, whenever people went to buy new policies, the cry of the day was "Buy term and invest the rest." This meant that people bought the cheaper-priced insurance policies and used the money they saved to invest in CD's or stocks or bonds or other high-yielding money vehicles.

To solve its own problem, the insurance industry created a hybrid policy known as universal life. These products allowed customers to buy term insurance and "invest the rest" all in *one* policy. The annual premiums were set once and were never adjusted upward or downward *and* the death benefit payment always stayed at the same amount. In these ways, the universal life policy was similar to a traditional whole-life policy. However, the rate of premium cost was not as high as whole-life rates had always been, so in that way it was like a traditional term policy.

The way this policy works is simple. It uses part of your annual premium payment to pay the insurance company for taking the risk that you might die that year and want a full payoff (as with term insurance); it uses the rest of your annual premium payment to invest in an interest-earning account (which could be a mutual fund or money market fund or stock portfolio). As you grow older and your risk of dying increases, your insurance company charges you more for the policy, but the extra payment comes from the interest you have been earning from the investment part of your policy. You pay no additional premiums (unless, of course, the investment side of your account has performed very poorly).

There are a number of reputable companies that currently sell universal life policies. Several of those known for their established equity investment accounts include Aetna Life Insurance and Annuity Company, Equitable Variable Life Insurance Company, New England Variable Life Insurance Company, and Kemper Investors Life Insurance Company.

Before buying from these or any other insurance companies, you should analyze three specific factors:

1. How much is the cost of the *term* insurance part of the premium, not just at your current age but also at all other ages?

2. What sort of earnings performance has the investment side of the fund had this past year and during the previous five- and ten-year cycles?

3. What are the sales charges, policy fees, and other expenses you will be responsible for both when you purchase the policy *and* decide to surrender it?

These important rates and points of data may not be readily apparent or available from a computer illustration or a sales brochure. In fact, some agents may not even carry this much supplemental information. Their computer-projected cash values will only be hypothetical and not guaranteed amounts. Be wary of any claims to continuous earnings higher than 9 percent yearly.

An annual report of an actual policy in force could be very revealing, if the agent or his home office will provide one. Financial stability and a company's rating should be considered. The point is that you should not base your choice on annual premium alone, since this could be misleading.

And, after all, this is something you're staking your life on! (See Figure 11, page 138.)

Financial—Planning Basics

All financial planning begins with a formula that reads like this: Total Earnings + Borrowed Money = All Living Expenses + All Accumulated Savings.

To figure the left side of the equation you tally all of your incoming cash (salary, bonuses, dividends, gifts, commissions, and all money received for loans on your house, car, furnishings, boat, and cottage, as well as loans taken out for paying off medical, college, and vacation debts).

To figure the right side of the equation you add up all the money you have in your savings and checking accounts, bonds and stocks, CD's and investment notes, real estate, gold jewelry and/or coins, and add this to all the money you must spend in order to meet the demands of your family budget.

If both sides of the equation match, you are an excellent money manager. If the left side is higher, you are working too much and are missing out on the joys of life or else you are borrowing so heavily that you will soon be overextended financially. However, if the right side is higher, then you are spending and saving money you have obtained on credit and this will rush you into financial disaster.

Income can be tax-deferred, tax-free, or taxable. Knowing the differences can assist you greatly in your estate planning.

Tax-deferred income refers to earnings you are now compounding which you will not pay tax on until a later time in life. For example, the money you put into an Individual Retirement Arrangement (IRA) will earn annual interest, but until you start drawing it out after age $59^{1}/_{2}$ you will not have to pay tax on those earnings.

Tax-free income is any money you receive or earn on which you will *never* have to pay taxes. For example, if someone chooses to give you a gift of $10,000 or less each year, that is not taxable. Your spouse can leave you all of his or her wealth and it will be tax-free. You are allowed to give away an inheritance of up to $600,000 to your children (or $1,200,000 as a couple) with no tax involvement. Earnings on certain municipal bonds are exempt from federal, state, city, and county taxes.

Taxable income is the cash you earn on which tax is due immediately upon receipt, such as your salary. That is why your taxes are usually withheld from your paycheck before you ever see that money.

Guarding Income During Bad Times

Since recessions, depressions, and eras of high inflation have become realities in modern America, they must be faced head-on. Prior to your death you must decide what kind of life you want to lead and then determine the amount of money it will take to meet your basic necessities and provide for the extras you desire in life. You must then determine how much wealth you wish to have available at the time of your death to pass on to your family members and favorite charities, while also having enough cash to pay taxes and final expenses. Having reached specific figures, it only remains to plan a strategy that will help you obtain those amounts.

Of course, saying what needs to be done is a lot easier than actually accomplishing it. The fact is that most people are pathetic money managers. Approximately 270,000 people will file bankruptcy every year during the 1990's. Literally millions of others will default on loans, have their purchases repossessed for lack of payment, lose their credit card privileges, go on welfare, seek food stamps in order to eat, and line up for unemployment benefits because they are virtually helpless when it comes to earning and/or managing money. Only one American in 100 dies wealthy; four others die in a state of being financially independent; the other 95 work until the day they die or live off relatives or other charities or the government, or else enter retirement at such a lowered rate of income that they must scale back on everything they do. This is sad, but true.

One financial counselor told me, "Too many people purchase things they don't actually need and charge them with cash they don't actually possess, in order to show off to folks they don't really like." Whether you are guilty of that "status purchasing" problem or not, here are three things worth spending some time thinking about.

1. *The responsibility to pay taxes.* The Bible tells us that kings and rulers are established by God, and that we must pay whatever tax we owe to our government in an ungrudging manner. Jesus taught His followers to

"render to Caesar the things that are Caesar's" (Matthew 22:21).

2. *The necessity to earn credit.* In Luke 16:10 we find Jesus teaching, "He who is faithful in what is least is faithful also in much." This is certainly true of credit dependability and cash management. If you want to be given a loan someday so that you can buy a large family van, make sure you don't miss any of the current payments on your little used compact car.

3. *The discipline of contentment.* The Bible reminds us that we should have the emotional, mental, and spiritual fortitude to be content with whatever we have rather than wasting our time daydreaming about what we lack. The apostle Paul wrote, "I have learned, in whatever state I am, to be content" (Philippians 4:11). If you take time to count your blessings, you'll discover that you're far better off than you thought.

Avoid Hoarding and Miserliness

Whereas estate planning is wise for all people, the Bible warns that it can be taken to extremes. The New Testament tells the story of a prosperous man who was so stingy that, rather than sharing his abundance with the poor, he tore down his little barns and built larger ones so that he could keep everything for himself. He died prematurely, however, and his earthly wealth was of no value to him when he stood before God to be judged.

A Christian who feels secure in his or her salvation knows that money can be used for better things than hoarding material items that will probably never be used. Adequate savings are important, but a secure soul is far more important. Any measures beyond that are subject to personal evaluation.

My feeling is that as Christians we should also be doing some estate planning for our home in glory. That too can be initiated now. It is wise to set giving goals for yourself each year. My wife and I use a "Faith Pledge and Giving Plan" which we designed shortly after getting married. We challenge ourselves to give above our current means, and through prayer and trust in God we strive to reach a donation goal for our church and other Christian organizations each year.

FAITH PLEDGE AND GIVING PLAN

I know that every good and great gift comes from God. As such, by God's grace and mercy, for the year 19_____ I pledge to give the following amounts of tithes and offerings to the noted ministries. If I am blessed with unexpected additional income, I will increase the amounts accordingly. I will pray faithfully for God to provide the money for me to reach each goal.

Signed _____

Dated _____

Home church tithe .... $_____
Donations to widows, orphans,
  and the poor .... $_____
Home missions and overseas missions ..... $_____
Contributions to a Christian day school ... $_____

Grand total for the year $_____

The purpose of this book has been twofold: First, to remind us that whatever we have on this earth is temporary and should have no merit when compared to an eternity in heaven; and second, to point out that God provides us with material blessings during our tenure on earth and that it is our responsibility to use proper stewardship in enjoying these blessings.

This book has provided you with a personal confession of how I misunderstood the responsibility of each Christian to care properly for his or her money and possessions. It has also provided you with the story of how I *did* learn this lesson and how it changed my life, both spiritually and financially. It is my fervent desire that once you have read this book and used its plans, suggestions, and methods, you too will be able to change your life. May God richly bless you in that endeavor!

ESTATE CAPITAL ANALYSIS
For

(Your Name Here)

19_____	Capital Requirements	19_____
$_____	Immediate cash requirements	$_____
$_____	Additional cash requirements	$_____
$_____	Other cash reqirements	$_____
	Invested capital required at _____% net annual return to provide	
$_____	$_____ per month permanent income	$_____
$_____	Discounted capital required to provide $_____ per month permanent income	$_____
$_____	$_____ per month temporary income for _____ years	$_____
$_____	Total capital requirements	$_____

Capital Assets

$_____	Cash	$_____
	Stocks & bonds (net sale value if these should be sold) (Capital gains tax)	$_____ $_____ $_____
$_____	Death benefit on a tax-qualified retirement plan	$_____
$_____	Personal property (net value)	$_____
$_____	Life insurance net estate value	$_____
$_____	Net value of real estate (Capital gains tax)	$_____ $_____
$_____	Other assets	$_____

Estate Capital Balance

$_____	Deficiency (–) or Surplus (+)	$_____

Figure 7

OBJECTIVES OF ESTATE PLANNING
For

<u>(Your Name Here)</u>

	19____	19____

Immediate Cash Requirements

	19____	19____
Funeral expenses	$_____	$_____
Final illness	$_____	$_____
Debt retirement	$_____	$_____
Probate costs	$_____	$_____
Estate taxes	$_____	$_____
Total	$_____	$_____

Additional Cash Requirements

Emergency fund	$_____	$_____
Mortgage collection	$_____	$_____
College funds	$_____	$_____
Total	$_____	$_____

Income Requirements

Permanent (per month)	$_____	$_____
Temporary (_____ years at _____ per month)	$_____	$_____

Other Cash or Income Requirements

Other dependents	$_____	$_____
Charitable bequests (church, schools)	$_____	$_____

Legal Documents Secured

Will
Trusts

Figure 8

INCOME TAX ANALYSIS

	Last Year	Estimated This Year
Income		
Salary and bonuses	_____	_____
Interest and dividends	_____	_____
Business Income (Schedule C)	_____	_____
State tax refund	_____	_____
Schedule D income	_____	_____
Schedule E income	_____	_____
Other	_____	_____
Gross Income	_____	_____
Less Adjustments to Income		
IRA/Keogh plan	_____	_____
Business cash outlays	_____	_____
Married couple deduction	_____	_____
Other	_____	_____
Total Income	_____	_____
Less Itemized Deductions	_____	_____
Medical expenses (Beyond 7½ percent of AGI)		
Taxes	_____	_____
Interest on home (mortgage & margin acct.)	_____	_____
Contributions	_____	_____
Miscellaneous	_____	_____
Less zero bracket	(_____)	(_____)
Total Deductions	_____	_____
Less Exemptions	_____	_____
Taxable Income	_____	_____
Federal Income Tax	_____	_____
Plus Other Taxes:		
Self-employment tax	_____	_____
Other	_____	_____
Less Credits	(_____)	(_____)
Total Federal Tax	_____	_____
Total State Tax	_____	_____
Total Tax	_____	_____
Marginal Tax Rate	_____	_____
Effective Tax Rate	_____	_____

Figure 9

TAX SUMMARY ANALYSIS

Deductions, Withholdings, and Estimates	Monthly Withholdings	Quarterly Estimates	Total Paid Annually
Federal income tax	$_____	$_____	$_____
State, city, and county income taxes	$_____	$_____	$_____
Social Security tax	$_____	$_____	$_____
TOTAL TAX	$_____	$_____	$_____

Figure 10

LIFE INSURANCE RECORD SHEET

Company Name	Agent's Name	Issue Date	Policy Number	Type of Policy	Insured	Owner
Individual policies	———	———	———	———	———	———
Retirement plan policies	———	———	———	———	———	———
Business policies	———	———	———	———	———	———
Mortgage policies	———	———	———	———	———	———

(Additional Data to Be Noted)

Beneficiary	Option for waiver of premium	Face value	Cash value	Cash value borrowed	Loan interest rate	Annual premiums
———	———	———	———	———	———	———
———	———	———	———	———	———	———
———	———	———	———	———	———	———

Figure 11

Suggested Reading on
Money Management

Ammer, Christine. *The A to Z of Investing*. New York: Mentor Books, 1986.

Bohigan, Valerie. *How to Make Your Home-Based Business Grow*. New York: Signet Books, 1984.

Brabec, Barbara. *Homemade Money*. White Hall, Virginia: Betterway Publications, Inc., 1984.

Curtin, Richard T. *Running Your Own Show: Mastering the Basics of Small Business*. New York: Mentor Executive Library, 1983.

Engel, Louis, and Brendan Boyd. *How to Buy Stocks*. Boston: Little, Brown & Company, 1982.

Finkler, Stephen A. *The Complete Guide to Finance and Accounting for Nonfinancial Managers*. Englewood Cliffs, NJ: Prentice-Hall, Inc., 1983.

Gibbs, William T. *Coin World 1991 Guide to U.S. Coins*. New York: New American Library, 1991.

Heatter, Justin. *The Small Investor's Guide to Big Profits in the Stock Market*. New York: Signet Books, 1983.

Hensley, Dennis E. *Financial Stability for Today's Christians*. Anderson, Indiana: Warner Press, 1988.

Hicks, Tyler G. *How to Borrow Your Way to a Great Fortune*. West Nyack, New York: Parker Publishing Co., 1970.

Kishel, Gregory and Patricia. *How to Start, Run and Stay in a Business*. New York: John Wiley & Sons, 1981.

Marcum, David, and Robert Meier. *Ten Best IRA Investments*. Publications International Ltd., Canada, 1982.

Marcum, David, and James B. Powell. *Ten Best Investments from $1,000 to $5,000*. Publications International Ltd., Canada, 1986.

Mattlin, Everett B. *How Much Are You Worth?* New York: Dreyfus Publications, Ltd., 1972.

Miller, L.D. *Best Rated Retirement Investments*. Publications International Ltd., Canada, 1986.

Shaefer, Joseph L. *Bringing Home the Gold*. Homewood, IL: Dow-Jones Irwin Publishers, 1989.

Sherman, Michael. *Compound Interest Tables*. Chicago: Contemporary Books, Inc., 1979.

Wayner, Stephen A. *Buying Right: Getting Started*. New York: Signet, 1990.

Weinstein, Grace W. *The Lifetime Book of Money Management*. New York: New American Library, 1987.

Yeomans, William N. *1000 Things You Never Learned in Business School*. New York: Mentor Books, 1985.

ABOUT THE AUTHOR

Dennis Hensley holds A.A., B.A., M.A., and Ph.D. degrees in English. He is the author of more than 26 books, including *Positive Workaholism* (Bobbs-Merrill), *The Freelance Writer's Handbook* (Harper & Row), *Time Management for Active Christians* (Warner Press), and *Writing for Religious and Other Specialty Markets* (Broadman Publishers).

Dr. Hensley has served as a consultant and training specialist for dozens of America's leading corporations, including North American Van Lines, General Motors, ITT, Magnavox, Lincoln Life Insurance Company, and Indiana-Michigan Power Company. He has also served as a consultant to a variety of Christian organizations, including Youth for Christ International, the Billy Graham Evangelistic Association, Campus Crusade for Christ, and Immanuel Christian School.

More than 2000 of Dr. Hensley's articles and short stories have been published in such periodicals as *Reader's Digest, Pace, Writer's Digest, People, The War Cry, The Inspirational Writer, Solo, In Business, Leader's Magazine, Market Builder, Between Times, Young Ambassador, The Writer, Grit, Modern Bride, Stereo, Purpose, Contact,* and *The Baptist Bulletin,* and in such national newspapers as *The Indianapolis Star, The Detroit Free Press, The Cincinnati Enquirer,* and *The Philadelphia Enquirer.*

Other Good Harvest House Reading

WORKING AT HOME
by *Lindsey O'Connor*

What are mothers (or fathers) to do when they want to stay home with their children and yet need additional income to make ends meet? Home businesses are sprouting up all over the country as more and more people are finding a way to combine parenting and working without having to give up traditional family roles.

In *Working at Home*, Lindsey O'Connor, who started a home business out of her own desire to be home after the birth of her first child, helps you determine whether a home business is for you and how you can get one off the ground.

GOD'S BEST FOR MY LIFE
by *Lloyd John Ogilvie*

Not since Oswald Chambers' *My Utmost for His Highest* has there been such an inspirational yet easy-to-read devotional. Dr. Ogilvie provides guidelines for maximizing your prayer and meditation time.

THE DAILY BIBLE
New International Version
Compiled by *F. LaGard Smith*

Unlike any other Bible you have ever read, *The Daily Bible* allows you to read the Scriptures chronologically as a powerful, uninterrupted account of God's interaction with human history.

You will see events from Creation through Revelation unfold before you like an epic novel, conveniently organized into 365 sections for daily reading. Gain a better overall perspective of Scripture by reading the Bible in the order the events occurred from the widely acclaimed New International Version.

CLASSIC CHRISTIANITY
Life's Too Short to Miss the Real Thing!
by *Bob George*

In his down-to-earth style, Bob George shares the road back to joy and contentment in the Christian life. Clearly outlining the common pitfalls and misconceptions that hinder and rob so many Christians today, Bob confronts the question of why so many Christians start out as enthusiastic believers and then decide that Christianity doesn't "work" for them. He then provides the truth that will help Christians get back on track and stay there.

THE INTIMATE HUSBAND
by *Richard Furman*

The Intimate Husband is the account of one man's decision to regain the love of his wife and save his faltering marriage. Talking with successful husbands around the country, he found the tools to reestablish the intimacy God intended.

Dear Reader:

We would appreciate hearing from you regarding this Harvest House nonfiction book. It will enable us to continue to give you the best in Christian publishing.

1. What most influenced you to purchase *Money Wise*?
   - ☐ Author
   - ☐ Subject matter
   - ☐ Backcover copy
   - ☐ Recommendations
   - ☐ Cover/Title
   - ☐ _____

2. Where did you purchase this book?
   - ☐ Christian bookstore
   - ☐ General bookstore
   - ☐ Department store
   - ☐ Grocery store
   - ☐ Other

3. Your overall rating of this book:
   ☐ Excellent ☐ Very good ☐ Good ☐ Fair ☐ Poor

4. How likely would you be to purchase other books by this author?
   - ☐ Very likely
   - ☐ Somewhat likely
   - ☐ Not very likely
   - ☐ Not at all

5. What types of books most interest you?
   (check all that apply)
   - ☐ Women's Books
   - ☐ Marriage Books
   - ☐ Current Issues
   - ☐ Self Help/Psychology
   - ☐ Bible Studies
   - ☐ Fiction
   - ☐ Biographies
   - ☐ Children's Books
   - ☐ Youth Books
   - ☐ Other _____

6. Please check the box next to your age group.
   - ☐ Under 18
   - ☐ 18-24
   - ☐ 25-34
   - ☐ 35-44
   - ☐ 45-54
   - ☐ 55 and over

Mail to: Editorial Director
Harvest House Publishers
1075 Arrowsmith
Eugene, OR 97402

Name _____

Address _____

City _____ State _____ Zip _____

**Thank you for helping us to help you
in future publications!**